Frederick P. Spalding

Notes on the Testing of Hydraulic Cement

Frederick P. Spalding

Notes on the Testing of Hydraulic Cement

ISBN/EAN: 9783337405762

Printed in Europe, USA, Canada, Australia, Japan

Cover: Foto ©Andreas Hilbeck / pixelio.de

More available books at **www.hansebooks.com**

NOTES

ON

THE TESTING AND USE

OF

HYDRAULIC CEMENT

BY

FRED P. SPALDING,

Assistant Professor of Civil Engineering,
Cornell University, Ithaca, N. Y.

ITHACA, N. Y.,
ANDRUS & CHURCH,
1893.

PREFACE.

THESE notes are designed for use as a text in a short course of instruction, as well as to serve the purpose of a hand book in the laboratory. In the first three chapters, an attempt has been made to give a brief statement of the general properties and characteristics of hydraulic cement, and its behavior under the more common contingencies of use, with a discussion of the various tests which may be applied to it, including both the ordinary tests of practice and the more elaborate ones which have been proposed, or which are in use in the larger experimental laboratories.

An effort has been made to give the best and most recent practice in cement testing, to point out the precautions necessary in making tests of quality, and to show the limitations within which the results of such tests may be considered as demonstrating the value of the material.

In the fourth chapter is given a selected list of recent periodical literature relating to the subject, with topical references to the various articles, intended to facilitate the work of those desiring to more fully investigate any of the divisions of the subject, and especially to aid students engaged in original or independent research.

References to authorities have not usually been given in the text, the list of literature in chapter IV seeming to render them unnecessary. To many of the papers there mentioned the author is indebted for information and suggestions.

F. P. S.

ITHACA, N. Y.,
Sept. 9, 1893.

CONTENTS.

CHAPTER I.

NATURE AND PROPERTIES OF CEMENT

CHAPTER II.

CEMENT TESTING.

CHAPTER III.

THE USE OF CEMENT.

CHAPTER IV.

LITERATURE RELATING TO CEMENT.

THE TESTING AND USE

— OF —

HYDRAULIC CEMENT.

CHAPTER I.

NATURE AND PROPERTIES OF CEMENT.

ART. I. DEFINITION.

When a limestone, composed of nearly pure carbonate of lime, is burned, the resulting mass of quicklime possesses the property of breaking up, or *slaking*, upon being treated with a sufficient quantity of water. The slaking of the lime is due to its rapid hydration when in contact with water. The process of slaking is accompanied by a considerable increase in the volume of the mass of lime, which is reduced to powder, and by a rise in temperature.

The powdered lime thus formed possesses the further property, when mixed to a paste with water and allowed to stand in air, of gradually hardening and firmly adhering to any surface with which it may be in contact. The hardening of nearly pure limes, which will occur only when in contact with air, is due to the formation of carbonate of lime by the absorption of carbonic acid from the air, together with a crystallizing of the hydrate from solution as the mortar dries out.

If the lime have, mixed or in combination with it, more than about 10 per cent. of impurities, its power of slaking is greatly lessened, if not entirely lost. If these impurities be of an inert description, the lime also loses to some extent its power of hardening, and is then known as poor or meagre lime. If the impurities in the lime be composed mainly of silica and alumina, they may, while lessening or destroying its property of slaking, impart to it the power to harden under water. The ability to harden in water is usually due to the formation of certain silicates and aluminates of lime during the process of burning, which possess the property of solidifying when hydrated by contact with water.

When the proportions of silica and alumina in the lime are such that the lime possesses the property of hardening in water, without having entirely lost that of slaking, the material is known as *hydraulic lime*.

When the acquirement of hydraulic properties has been accompanied by an entire loss of the property of slaking, the product is an *hydraulic cement*.

Hydraulic·limes and cements may be made

either by burning limestones containing the proper proportions of hydraulic ingredients, in which case they are known as *natural* limes or cements, or by the admixture of material containing such ingredients to the limestone before burning, or to the lime afterward, when they are known as *artificial* limes or cements.

The hydraulic properties of a lime or cement vary, within certain limits, according to the proportion of hydraulic ingredients contained by them, and the ratio of the weight of silica and alumina to that of the lime in the material is known as its *hydraulic index*. For hydraulic limes, the hydraulic index may vary from about $\frac{10}{100}$ to $\frac{40}{100}$. For cements it is usually between $\frac{40}{100}$ and $\frac{70}{100}$, but is sometimes higher.

Hydraulic limes are used in some parts of Europe, but are not manufactured to any extent in this country. The American cement industry is, however, growing to very large proportions, and cement of all grades is extensively made, although large quantities of high grade foreign cements are still imported.

ART. 2. PORTLAND CEMENT.

The term *Portland Cement* is commonly used to designate an hydraulic cement formed by burning to the point of vitrifaction, a mixture of limestone and clay in proper proportions, and reducing the resulting mass to powder by grinding. The production of a good Portland cement requires great care in manufacture ; the chemical composition must the accurate ; the mixture of the stone and clay must be thorough and uniform, and the burning must be complete.

The action of the cement seems to depend upon the formation, during the burning, of the silicate and aluminate of lime, the other elements being considered in the light of impurities, although some of them may at times be of service in the cement.

The hydraulic index of Portland Cement varies from about $\frac{42}{100}$ to $\frac{50}{100}$, and its normal composition is usually practically within the limits given below.

Silica, ... 20 per cent. to 25 per cent.
Alumina, . . . 5 "   "   " 8 "   "
Iron Oxide, . . 2 "   "   " 4 "   "
Lime, ... 58 "   "   " 65 "   "
Magnesia, . . . 0.5 "   "   " 2 "   "
Sulphuric Acid, 0.5 "   "   " 1 "   "

If in mixing the ingredients too great a quantity of clay be used, the surplus will remain in the cement as inert material, causing a weakening of its action. If the surplus of clay be considerable and the burning thorough, the material may be reduced to powder in the burning, producing a cement of comparative little value.

When the cement is formed with too small a proportion of clay, the excess of lime remains in it as free lime and constitutes one of the chief dangers in the use of cement, as, although it will not prevent the proper action of the cement when used, a very small percentage of free lime may be sufficient to cause the mortar to afterward swell and become cracked and distorted. This is due to the increase of volume caused by the slaking of the lime by the water. When the free lime is in very small quantity the slaking will not take place until after the hardening of the mortar, and then becomes a strong disrupting force.

Professor Le Chatelier, who has made a very careful study of the nature and action of Portland cement, gives two limits within which the quantity of lime in the cement must always be found. These are, that the proportion of lime should always be greater than that represented by the formula :

$$\text{I.} \quad \frac{CaO + MgO}{SiO_2 - Al_2O_3 - FeO_3} = 3.$$

In which the symbols represent the number of equivalents of the substances present, and that it should never exceed that given by the formula:

$$\text{2.} \quad \frac{CaO + MgO}{SiO_2 + Al_2O_3 - FeO} = 3$$

This is based upon the theory that the essential ingredients of the cement are the silicate of lime of formula $3CaO, SiO_2$, the aluminate of lime of formula $3CaO, Al_2O_3$, and the silico aluminate of formula $3CaO, Al_2O_3, 2SiO_2$. Of these, the first two are the active elements of the cement, the third being inert in the cement, but being first formed in the burning and acting as a flux to facilitate the combination of the silica and lime.

Formula 1 represents the point at which the amount of lime present would be just sufficient to form the tricalcic silicate and the silico-aluminate, no aluminate being formed. If less lime than this be present the bicalcic silicate ($2CaO, SiO_2$) would be formed, which powders upon cooling in the furnace and does not possess the power of hardening in contact with water.

Formula 2 represents the point at which the amount of lime would be sufficient to form the tricalcic silicate and tricalcic aluminate, to the exclusion of the silico aluminate. If more lime than this be present it will remain in the form of free lime. It is necessary to keep well within these limits as the mixture will necessarily be somewhat imperfect.

It is also stated by Professor Le Chatelier that for Portland cement of good quality formula 1 usually gives 3.5 to 4 and formula 2 gives 2.5 to 2.7 as a result.

Free lime in the cement may also result from the lack of uniformity in the incorporation of the ingredients, or from underburning. In this case the process of combination is not complete, and the free lime and bicalcic silicate may exist at the same time in the cement.

ART 3. NATURAL CEMENT.

Natural cements are those which are made by burning a limestone which naturally contains the proportions of silica and other ingredients necessary to cause it to harden under water when made into mortar.

These cements are now made in considerable quantities in many places throughout this country, and differ very widely in composition and value. As in the case of a Portland cement, the making of a good natural cement implies care in the selection of materials, and frequently the admixture of various portions of the rock used is necessary to the production of a cement of uniformly good quality. The one class may thus merge into the other, and the classification of some becomes doubtful.

There is considerable confusion in the use of terms to designate the various kinds of natural cement. In general they may be disiinguished in this country by a name derived from the locality in which they are manufactured, but greater uniformity of nomenclature would be advantageous as conducing to a better understanding of the characteristics of the material.

American natural cements may perhaps be divided into three general classes, natural Portland cements, magnesian cements and aluminous cements.

Those natural cements which possess about the normal composition of an artificial Portland cement are sometimes designated *natural Portland cements*. In Europe cements of this character are usually grouped under the name of slow setting natural cements. In common with nearly all natural cements, these possess usually a higher hydraulic index than the artificial Portland cements. They show in general characteristics similar to those of the artificial Portlands, and are usually more heavily burned than other grades of natural cement.

The *magnesian cements* are those in which a portion of the lime of the Portland is replaced by magnesia. These cements are also lighter burned and have a higher hydraulic index than Portland cements. The *Rosendale cements* are a class of natural cements made from a magnesian limestone found abundantly along the Hudson River. The term *Rosendale* is sometimes applied in a general way to all American natural cements, but it is more properly restricted to those from the locality of the lower Hudson, and of the magnesian variety.

The composition and characteristics of cement of this class vary considerably, even in the same locality, according to the strata from which the rock is obtained and the care used in selecting and manipulating it. The quantity of magnesia in it varies from about 10 per cent to 25 per cent. The Utica cements of Illinois also belong to this class, with several other Western makes.

Cements of the *aluminous* variety are known in Europe as quick setting natural cements, or Roman cements. They differ from Portland cement in having a higher hydraulic index, and in containing more alumina. They also usually contain a higher percentage of sulphuric acid than the other varieties, but not always. The Louisville cements may be placed in this class.

Between these two latter classes of cements, are a number of varieties which gradually merge the one into the other. These contain a higher percentage both of alumina and of magnesia than the Portlands. They are widely scattered throughout the country and vary greatly in their composition and characteristics, some being noticably low in their amount of lime, and others containing considerable quantities of iron oxide.

To this general description the larger number of
American natural cements belong.

ART. 4. SLAG CEMENT.

Slag cements are those formed by an admixture
of slaked lime with ground blast furnace slag.
The slag used has approximately the composition
of an hydraulic cement, being composed mainly
of silica and alumina, and lacking a proper proportion of lime to render it active as a cement. In
preparing the cement, the slag upon coming from
the furnace is plunged into water and reduced to
a spongy form from which it may be readily
ground. This is dried and ground to a fine
powder. The powdered slag and slaked lime are
then mixed in proper proportions and ground
together, so as to very thoroughly distribute them
through the mixture. It is of first importance in
a slag cement that the slag be very finely ground
and that the ingredients be very uniformly and
intimately incorporated into the mixture.

Both the composition and methods of manufacture of slag cements vary considerably in
different places. They usually contain a higher
percentage of alumina than Portland cements,
and the materials are in a different state of combination, as, being mixed after the burning,
the silicates and aluminates of lime formed

during the burning of Portland cement cannot exist in slag cement.

Other mixed cements are sometimes made in Europe using different material of the same general nature as the slag. Puzzuolana cements are those made by a mixture of volcanic ashes with lime, although the name is sometimes applied to mixed cements in general. The use of puzzuolana has been known for many years in Europe, and dates back to the time of the Romans. A volcanic earth called trass is also frequently employed for this purpose. The slag cements are, however, the only important ones of this nature, the others being of limited application.

ART. 5. SETTING OF CEMENT.

When cement powder is mixed with water to a plastic condition, and allowed to stand, it gradually combines into a solid mass, taking the water into combination, and soon becomes firm and hard. This process of combination amongst the particles of the cement is known as the *setting* of the cement.

Cements of different composition differ very widely in their rate and manner of setting. Some occupy but a few minutes in the operation, and others require several hours. Some begin setting immediately and take considerable time to com-

plete the set, while others stand for a considerable time with no apparent action and then set very quickly.

The points where the set is said to begin and end are necessarily arbitrarily fixed, and are differently determined, usually by trying when the mortar will sustain a needle carrying a given weight. The point at which the set is supposed to begin is when the stiffening of the mass first becomes perceptible, and the end of set is when the cohesion extends through the mass sufficiently to offer such resistance to any change of form, as to cause rupture before any perceptible deformation can take place.

It is sometimes stated that the chemical change involved in setting is an instantaneous occurrence at about the time we call the beginning of set, and that the gradual hardening then begins and is a continuous process until the maximum strength is reached. However this may be, with some cements a quite noticable change suddenly shows itself at about this time, in the disappearance of water from the surface of the mortar and the sudden stiffening of the mass.

Professor Le Chatelier in his study of Portland cements explains the phenomena of setting, by showing that certain salts, including the aluminate and silicate of lime which form the active elements of Portland cement, are much more soluble in an anhydrous than in a hydrated condition.

When they first come into contact with water, as in mixing the mortar, the anhydrous salt enters at once into saturated solution. In a short time by contact with the water the salt becomes hydrated, and the hydrated salt being less soluble is precipitated in a crystalline form.

With the aluminate of lime this action is especially rapid, and therefore as might be expected cements containing considerable proportions of this salt are more quick setting than others ; cements with a low hydraulic index are apt to be quicker setting than those of the same class with a high one ; cements with a considerable proportion of alumina to silica are apt to be quicker setting than those with a less one. It is to be observed however, that an analysis of a cement giving the elements of its composition does not show the state of combination, and nothing can be necessarily inferred from a knowledge of such composition as to its action in setting. Thus, an underburned cement will set more quickly than the same cement thoroughly burned, and slag cement, while usually showing a high percentage of alumina, is generally slow in setting.

It is not correct to state as is commonly done that natural cement is quick setting and Portland cement slow setting. The aluminous natural cements are commonly quick setting, though not always so, as those with a high hydraulic index or containing a considerable percentage of sulphuric acid may set quite slowly. The magnesian and Portland varieties may be either quick or slow. Specimens of either variety may be had that will set at any rate, from the slowest to the most rapid, and no distinction can be drawn between the various classes in this regard.

The age of a cement affects the rate of setting to some extent. This is especially liable to be the case with quick setting cements when they are exposed to dry air. Such exposure makes the setting slower. A slow setting cement of good quality is generally less affected, if affected at all. When the air to which cement is exposed is quite moist it may gradually absorb water until it is practically ruined, and will not set at all. Where the cement is kept in tight barrels, its age is not usually of so much consequence, unless it be exposed to dampness, which may penetrate the barrels and cause it to become hard prematurely.

Fine grinding, to some extent, accelerates the setting of a cement.

The time occupied in setting is also affected by various external circumstances under which the cement is used. The effect upon different kinds of cement is very different in degree, old cements being generally less affected than fresh ones.

The quantity of water used in mixing the mortar is one of the most important conditions, the less the quantity, provided there be sufficient to thoroughly dampen the mass of cement, the quicker will be the set. With some Portland cement, changing the quantity of water used in mixing neat cement from 20 per cent. to 25 per cent. of the weight of cement, will double or even triple the time necessary for the mortar to set. In other cases the effect is comparatively slight.

The nature of the water used in mixing may also affect the rate of setting. When sea water is used the setting is usually slower than with fresh water, the chloride and sulphate of magnesia being the principle retarding elements. Cements with a high hydraulic index will show a less difference between fresh and sea water than those of the same class with a low one, and well burned cements less than imperfectly burned ones. The experiments of M. Candlot indicate that this is due to the action of the salts mentioned above upon the aluminate of calcium, and that those cements containing the highest percentage of aluminate are affected the most, by being mixed with sea water.

Water containing sulphate of lime in solution retards the setting of cement. This fact has been made use of to some extent in Europe in the adulteration of cement, powdered gypsum being mixed with it to make it slow setting, greatly to the injury of the material.

The temperature of the water used in mixing has an important bearing upon the time required for setting, the higher the temperature, within certain limits, the more rapid the set. Many cements which require several hours to set when mixed with water at a temperature of 40° Fahr., will set in a few minutes if the temperature of the water be increased to 80° Fahr. Below a certain inferior limit, ordinarily from 30° to 40° Fahr., the mortar will not set, while at a certain upper limit, in many cements between 100° and 140° Fahr., a change is suddenly made from a very rapid to a very slow rate, which then continually decreases as the temperature increases, until practically the mortar will not set.

The temperature of the cement, and that of the air in which the mortar is placed during setting, influence the rate of setting in about the same manner as that of the water. In case the air in which the mortar is placed be dry, the setting will usually be somewhat more rapid than if it be moist, and if it be too dry, the rapid evaporation of the water from the surface of the mortar may cause drying cracks in the mortar.

Quick setting cements usually show a rise of

temperature during setting, due to the rapidity of the action which takes place. It has been suggested that the time occupied by the setting would be better shown by observing the period of advanced temperature, than by noting the stiffening of the mortar, as is now done. Most slow setting cements however do not show sufficient change of temperature, if any takes place, to be appreciable, and the rise of temperature, where it does take place, may not in all cases be the result of the process of setting.

ART. 6. HARDENING OF CEMENT.

After the completion of the setting of the cement, the mortar continues to increase in cohesive strength over a considerable period of time, and this subsequent development of strength is called the *hardening* of the cement.

The process of hardening appears to be quite distinct from, and independent of that of setting. A slow setting cement is apt, after the first day or two, to gain strength more rapidly than a quick setting one, but it does not necessarily do so. The ultimate strength of the cement also, is quite independent of the rate of setting. A cement imperfectly burned will set more quickly and gain less ultimate strength than the same cement when properly burned, but of two cements of different composition the quicker setting may be the stronger.

There is as wide a variation in the rate of hardening attained by different cements as in the rate of setting ; some gain strength rapidly and attain their ultimate strength in a few days, while others harden more slowly at first and continue to gain in strength for several years. The rate of early hardening gives but little indication of the ultimate action of the cement, as the final strength of the mortar may be the same, however rapidly the strength is attained. Portland cement usually hardens more rapidly and gains its maximum strength more quickly than natural cement, and also as a rule the Portland cement will attain greater strength when used in the same manner. Of two cements of the same class, however, it is not safe to infer that that which most rapidly gains strength will prove the stronger and more permanent material; in fact, where an abnormally high strength is shown in a few days, the presumption as to the probable final strength should be against the cement giving such result and in favor of one hardening at a more moderate rate.

The rate at which cement should harden for a given use, depends, of course, upon the necessity of developing early strength in the work. For many purposes, such as most sub-aqueous construction, such early strength is highly desirable if not necessary, but for most engineering work a very rapid hardening does not seem necessary and better results may often be obtained by the use of a material of more gradual action.

Cements with a low hydraulic index commonly harden more rapidly than those with a high one. When the material is somewhat *over-clayed* the hardening becomes slow, and if this effect be considerable, the material shows a very low early strength and is commonly considered worthless, but may continue to gain in strength over a very long period and ultimately make a hard and durable mortar.

Where the cement is *overlimed* it is likely to gain strength very rapidly in the beginning, and later to lose its strength, or, if the percentage of free lime be sufficient it will ultimately disintegrate. When the mortar is immersed in sea water this disintegrating action is more rapid than when it is kept in fresh water.

Finely ground cements, mixed neat, will harden more rapidly than when coarsely ground, but will not usually reach so high a degree of final strength. When mixed with sand the fine cement will reach the greater strength.

Effect of Sand. Cement is generally used in a mortar mixed with a certain proportion of sand,

and the action of the mortar is necessarily largely affected by the nature and quantity of the sand used.

When the cement is finely ground and the sand of good quality, a mortar composed of equal parts of each will, as a general thing, finally attain a strength as high as, or higher than that of the neat cement. Cements of different characters, however, vary considerably in their power to take sand without loss of strength ; some of the weaker ones may not be able to take more than half their weight of standard sand, while others can be mixed with considerably more than their own weight, without loss of strength at the end of twelve months after mixing. All have a certain limit within which they may be made stronger by an admixture of good sand than they would be if mixed neat.

Cement mixed with sand will always harden more slowly than neat cement, and require a much longer time to attain its maximum strength. As the proportion of sand to cement is increased both the rate of hardening and final strength of the mortar are diminished.

The finer ground the cement, the greater will be its resistance when mixed with sand, both in the earlier and later stages, and also the sooner will it reach its ultimate strength. The effect of fine grinding is much greater where the proportion of sand to cement in the mortar is large, as the power of the cement to take sand without diminution of strength is thereby greatly increased. The coarser particles of the cement may be considered as practically inert material, which acts rather as sand than as cement in the mortar, and the power of the cement to harden and develop strength, when mixed with sand, is dependent upon the amount of fine material contained in it.

Clean and sharp sand will always give a higher strength in mortar than that containing an admixture of clay or earth, or that composed of rounded grains.

Coarse sand will also give greater strength than that which is very fine.

Quantity and Nature of Water. When the quantity of water used in mixing is sufficient to reduce the mortar to a soft condition, the hardening as well as the setting becomes more slow, and the strength during the early period is much less, than if a less quantity be used. This difference in strength disappears to some extent with time, and the mortar mixed wet may eventually gain nearly as much strength as though mixed with less water.

When the quantity of water used is not sufficient to reduce the mass to a plastic condition, the mortar will not be so thoroughly compacted, and will not reach the same strength as when made plastic, unless pressure be applied to it. But if just sufficient water be used to thoroughly dampen the mortar, 'and pressure be applied to expel the air and close the voids, the early strength will be greater than when more water is used. This difference, like the former one, disappears to a certain extent with time, but the final strength is usually greater with the less quantity of water.

Mortar kept immersed in sea water usually hardens more rapidly than that kept in fresh water. This difference is commonly much more noticable with neat cement than with mortar containing considerable proportions of sand.

Cements with a low hydraulic index show the greatest difference between sea and fresh water.

Cements containing small quantities of free lime give much greater early strength in sea than in fresh water, but are also sooner disintegrated by the sea water.

The nature of the water with which the mortar is mixed is not of so great importance as that of the water in which it is allowed to harden. When the mortar is to be kept in air, the nature of the water used in mixing becomes more important, although probably the variations in ordinary natural water are rarely sufficient to produce any appreciable difference in the strength of the mortar.

Cement kept under water hardens more rapidly

at first than that exposed to the air, but usually, that kept in air will ultimately reach greater strength. The highest strength will ordinarily be produced by keeping the cement during the early period in water or at least in very moist air, and later in dry air. Nearly any cement mortar will harden more rapidly and attain greater strength if kept moist during the operation of setting and the period of early hardening than if it be exposed at that time to dry air.

Effect of Temperature. The temperature of the water with which cement mortar is mixed has a quite appreciable effect both upon its rate of hardening and its ultimate strength, and the temperature of the air at the time of mixing has a similar effect. The lower the temperature at which the mixing is done, the slower will be the hardening, and the greater will the final strength be. This difference is not sufficient to be important at ordinary air temperatures in so far as the use of the mortar is concerned, but is quite appreciable in making comparative tests.

If the air at time of mixing be sufficiently cold to freeze the mortar before it can set, it will not set while frozen, but most cements will do so after thawing out, and but few of them will be injured by such freezing in so far as their strength is concerned.

The temperature of the air or water in which the mortar is immersed during the time of hardening has a very appreciable effect upon the rate of hardening of many cements. This effect differs very radically for different material; with some the process is greatly accelerated by keeping them hot as compared with what would be the result in cold air or water; others are not appreciably affected, while still others seem to be retarded in their hardening by the application of heat. This variation is to be found among cements of the same class, and is seemingly independent of their value. Cements with a low hydraulic index usually show the greatest gain in rate of hardening under the action of heat·

ART. 7. ADHESION.

For most of the ordinary uses to which cement mortar is put, its power of adhering to the surfaces with which it is placed in contact is of greater consequence than is its ·cohesive strength. This power of adhering to other material is very highly developed in a good cement, but its exact evaluation is a matter of considerable difficulty on account of the many circumstances that may operate to affect it. It has been found in general that the cohesive and adhesive strengths vary in somewhat the same manner for different material, and the determination of cohesive strength is commonly relied upon as a test of value.

The strength of a mortar composed of cement and sand, calls into play the adhesion of the cement to the sand as well as the cohesive strength of the cement itself, and the larger the proportion of sand the greater the dependence upon adhesion. An idea of the value of the adhesive power of the cement may therefore be obtained by observing the comparative strengths of mortar made from neat cement, and that composed of cement and sand in varying proportions.

The adhesion of mortar to any surface to which it may be applied will depend upon the nature and condition of the surface, being greater as the material is more hard and non-porous. The adhesive strength unlike the cohesive strength will be greater as the mortar is made more wet, or when mortar of ordinary consistency is in use, the adhesive strength will be greater if the surface to which it is to be applied is first thoroughly dampened.

The *fineness* of the cement has an important effect upon adhesive strength, the finer the cement the greater its adhesive strength. A mortar composed of cement and sand will also possess greater power of adherence when coarse sand is used than when the sand is fine.

ART. 8.   PERMANENCE OF VOLUME OR SOUNDNESS.

The permanence of any structure, erected by
the use of cement, is dependent upon the power of
the cement, after the setting and hardening pro-
cesses are complete, to retain its strength and form
unimpaired over an indefinite period. Experiment has shown that mortars made from cement
of good quality frequently continue to gain in
strength and hardness through a period of several
years, or at least that there is no material diminution of strength with time, and that changes of
temperature, or in the degree of moisture sur-
rounding it, produce no injurious effect upon the
material.   This durability of the material in use is
commonly known as the *permanence* of *volume* or
the *soundness* of the cement.

Heat has the same effect to expand and contract
cement mortar of good quality as it has upon other
materials.   The coefficient of expansion for neat
Portland cement mortar according to a series of
experiments at "l'Ecole des Ponts et Chaussees,"
is about the same as that of iron.   For sand
mortar the coefficient is somewhat less.

When mortar which has been immersed in
water is transferred to dry air, a slight contraction
may take place in volume, together with an increase in strength, while a transferrence the
other way may produce the opposite result, but
no distortion of form or disintegration of the

mortar will take place in either case if the cement be of good quality.

Sometimes cement when made into mortar sets and hardens properly, and later, when exposed to the action of the atmosphere or water, becomes distorted and cracked, or even entirely disintegrated. If the composition deviates but slightly from the normal, this process of disintegration may not show itself for a considerable time and proceeds very slowly. It thus becomes an element of considerable danger as it is liable to escape detection in testing the cement. The most common cause of this unsoundness is probably the existence of small quantities of free lime or magnesia in the cement. Magnesia in Portland cement is from this cause always an element of danger, and should not be present in a quantity exceeding about 3 per cent. In many natural cements, however, magnesia replaces a portion of the lime when the cement is of normal composition, and does not render the cement unsound, unless, like the lime, it is in excess.

The presence of sulphate of lime in any considerable quantity also commonly produces unsoundness in the cement, and for that reason an analysis of the cement should usually show but a very small percentage of sulphuric acid ; for Portland cement, the limit is about one per cent. There are, however, cements in which a larger percentage of sulphate occurs normally and does not produce unsoundness ; these are, according to M. Candlot, usually the ones containing a high percentage of alumina.

The presence of aluminate of lime is also said to be a cause of unsoundness where cement mortar is to be used in sea water, and Portland cement for such use should contain as high a percentage of silica in proportion to the alumina as possible.

With most unsound cements the disintegrating action is more rapid at high than at low temperatures. Sea water usually causes more rapid disintegration than fresh water.

The term, *permanence of volume*, if limited to the power of the material to resist actual change of form, or dimension, in the body of mortar, is not necessarily synonomous with *soundness*, if, by soundness, we designate its power to resist disintegration over a long period. Most unsound cements fail by swelling and cracking, after which disintegration occurs. This is especially apt to be the case with those containing an appreciable percentage of free lime or magnesia, the failure occurring in a comparatively short time. In some other cements, however, the failure occurs by a gradual softening of the mass of mortar, without appreciable change of form or dimension, the process being very slow, sometimes not noticeable for several months after the mortar is mixed.

CHAPTER II.

METHODS OF TESTING CEMENT.

ART. 9. OBJECT OF TESTING.

The testing of cement usually differs from the testing of other materials of construction, in that the test is intended to determine whether the material tested be of good quality, and not as a measure of its actual strength in use. Cement is not commonly employed where it is subjected to stresses nearly approaching its limit of safe strength, and a knowledge of just what that strength may be, is not ordinarily of so much consequence. What we want to know about the cement is that it will set and harden into a solid mass, which will firmly adhere to any surface with which it may be in contact, and that it will endure through a long time, without change of form or loss of solidity.

As ordinary tests must be made in a short time, but a few days at most being usually allowed for determining the quality of the material, the problem to be met in testing is to apply such tests, as will enable a prediction to be made, from its behavior under them in a short time, what it will do in a long time under the circumstances of its use. The difficulty of this with a material varying so widely in its character, and in its behavior under various conditions, is evident. If we have a particular brand of cement whose characteristics we know, we may readily determine whether a given sample is of normal quality, and predict something of its future from its behavior under short time tests. Very little, however, can be done in the way of generalization, and for a new or unknown material we can only state a somewhat indefinite probability as to final results.

Tests may be imposed which in nearly all cases will secure good material, but at the expense many times of rejecting equally good or better material. This, however, will be unavoidable until such time as the characteristics of the various makes of cement are more fully known, and the tests to which each should be subjected better understood. The individuality of the cement is a very important factor.

The tests, which are usually imposed to determine the quality of hydraulic cement, are those of weight, fineness, time of setting, tensile strength and soundness. Chemical analysis is sometimes made, and specific gravity test is substituted for that of weight, or both are frequently omitted. Compression tests are also sometimes added.

The greatest weight is usually given to the test of tensile strength, and much greater value is

commonly placed upon the results of that test
than they deserve. It is much the simplest and
best means of making a test for strength, and is
very desirable as showing the proper hardening
of the mortar, but cements cannot be graded in
value by the strength attained in a short time.
A cement giving a very high early strength is to
be relied upon, only in so far, as it has been
shown by experience capable of subsequently
maintaining such strength. The attempt to produce a cement, which will develop great strength
in a short time, is liable to result in a lowering of
the hydraulic index, and frequently in the presence of free lime, giving a material more likely to
be unsound than one of more moderate strength.

The test for soundness or permanence of volume
is a very important one, as giving an indication
of the probable durability of the material, but in
this as in all other cases, a knowledge of the normal action of the material will contribute greatly
to the proper interpretation of the test.

The test for fineness is also important as showing the power of the cement to take sand.

It is recommended by the Committee of the
American Society of Civil Engineers upon a uniform system of testing, that tests for quality be
limited to the above three most important tests,
fineness, tensile strength and soundness, and this
recommendation is now commonly followed in

this country, although the test for soundness as usually made is of little value.

The determination of the weight of a given volume of the cement to be tested, is frequently made for the purpose of obtaining an idea as to whether the cement is properly burned. An underburned cement is somewhat lighter in weight than if thoroughly burned.

The weight of the cement will also depend upon the fineness to which it is ground, the coarser the particles of the cement the heavier it will be ; therefore when a weight test is included in a specification, a test for fineness must also be included, to prevent the attainment of weight by coarse grinding.

The weight test is not now commonly employed in tests for quality, as it is indefinite both in its execution and in the interpretation of its results, and other tests are of more importance in determining the value of the material.

As the cement powder may be packed so as to give very different weights for the same volume, it is necessary to use a uniform system of filling the measure in determination of weight. The common method of conducting the test is, to sift the powder through a coarse sieve and allow it to fall through a funnel or down an inclined slide through a given height into the measure The height of fall and the size of the measure will both affect the result, the cement packing closer in a large than in a small measure.

In France the standard method of testing weight is to sift the cement through a sieve of 5000 meshes per square centimeter, and weigh only the powder which passes that sieve. After passing the sieve, the powder falls upon a metal slide, or square trough, one-half meter long and inclined at an angle of 45° with the horizontal. The material slides down this trough and into a measure holding a litre, the top of which is placed one centimeter below the bottom of the trough. When full the measure is struck and weighed.

The advantage of this method is that it makes the weight to a certain extent independent of fineness. In American and English practice there has been no uniformity in the methods employed in different laboratories for determining weight.

The ordinary weight of Portland cement varies from 70 to 100 pounds per cubic foot. Natural cements are usually somewhat lighter.

The determination of specific gravity is often substituted for that of volume weight, and is a better guide to a knowledge of actual density. The differences of specific gravity are, however, so small as to require very accurate determinations of its value.

The specific gravity of Portland cement of good quality varies from 3.05 to 3.20 and is usually above 3.10. That of natural cement varies from about 2.70 to 3.10. A difference in density may be caused by variation in composition, as well as in the degree of calcination of the material, and therefore the greater density does not of necessity represent the best preparation of the cement.

The test for specific gravity is commonly made by immersing a known weight of the cement in a liquid which will not act upon it, and obtaining its volume by observing the rise in the surface of the liquid.

Care must be taken in immersing the cement to permit the escape of the air bubbles contained in it, either by sifting the powder through the liquid, or if the powder be first placed in the apparatus and the liquid afterward introduced, by agitating until the liquid is thoroughly distributed through the cement and then allowing the mass to settle.

If a tube graduated to cubic centimeters be enlarged to a ball at its lower end, or be attached to a dish at its lower end, and this tube be filled with benzine to a height at which a reading may be taken on the tube, and a given weight of cement (as 100 grammes) be sifted through the tube into the dish or ball below, and a second reading taken on the tube at the surface of the liquid, the difference between the two readings will be the actual volume of cement in cubic centimeters, then, weight in grammes divided by volume in centimeters gives directly the specific gravity. The Schuman Volumenometer works upon this principle. Several other forms use a somewhat similar apparatus, but first place the cement in the apparatus, then pour a known quantity of liquid over it, depending upon agitating the apparatus sufficiently to eliminate the air bubbles from the cement powder.

ART. II. TEST FOR FINENESS.

The fineness to which a cement is ground is always a matter of importance, as upon it depends very greatly the adhesive power of the cement, and its ability to take sand. A test for fineness is nearly always given in specifications for cement, and this test is of most importance when, as is very commonly the case, the tensile strength is tested for neat cement only. In this case, the attainment of a proper strength neat, together with a fair degree of fineness, practically insures that the cement will give good results when used with sand.

The fineness which should be required in a cement is largely a question of relative economy ; the finer ground the cement, the larger the quan-

tity of sand that may legitimately be used with
it. All the coarse parts of the cement are to be
considered as inert material, or practically as a
certain amount of sand already mixed with the
cement, and the problem, in deciding upon a requirement as to fineness, may become that of
determining whether it will be cheaper to pay a
higher price for the cement, or use more of it.

The test for fineness simply consists in sifting
the cement through a sieve, or a set of sieves,
and observing the amount retained by each sieve.

The committee of the American Society of Civil
Engineers upon standard tests, recommend the
use of sieves of 2500, 5476, and 10000 meshes per
square inch.   Specifications usually, however,
require only a single sieve, generally that of 2500
meshes, but sometimes that of 10000 meshes.   A
more general use of the finer sieve would undoubtedly be advantageous, as it is now generally
admitted that all material coarser than that dimension is practically inert, and a real measure
of useful fineness is not given by the 2500 mesh
sieve.   A common requirement is, that not more
than 10 per cent. by weight of the cement be retained upon a sieve of 2500 meshes, or that not
more than 20 per cent. be retained upon that of
10000 meshes, or both.   Most of the cements
commonly in use in this country easily comply
with these requirements ; many of the best ones

do not give a residue on the coarse sieve of more
than 1 to 3 per cent., or on the fine one of more
than 8 to 12 per cent., natural cements being
usually finer than Portland. Some brands of
Portland cement, however, seem to be prepared
with special reference to meeting the requirement
of the 2500 mesh sieve, and are very coarse when
tested with a finer one.

In France and Germany sieves of 324, 900 and
5000 meshes per square centimeter are employed.
The present requirements in Germany and
Switzerland are that not more than 15 per cent
shall be retained on the sieve of 900 meshes per
square centimeter.

The size of wire of which the sieve is made is
of course important as regulating the size of
openings and should always be stated, the common standard is that the diameter of the wire
should be about $\frac{1}{3}$ of the spacing between
centers. It is not commonly possible to get
sieves with perfect regularity either of spacing or
diameter of wires, a sufficiently near approx-
imation for practical work may be obtained
by using care in selecting the sieve, but the
gauze frequently offered for this use differs very
widely in the sizes of openings for the same number per inch, and sometimes the openings are
quite irregular in size in different parts of the
same sieve.

ART. 12. RATE OF SETTING.

The rate of setting of cement is tested for the purpose of determining if it be suitable for a given use, and not as a measure of the quality of the material. For most purposes, where immediate setting is not required to prevent disturbance of the mortar before hardening, the moderately slow setting cements are found more convenient, as they need not be handled so quickly and may be mixed in somewhat larger quantities.

Testing for time of setting consists in arbitrarily fixing two points in the process of consolidation which are called the beginning and the end of set. These points are differently determined in the different systems of testing.

The method recommended by the committee of the American Society of Civil Engineers is that proposed by General Gillmore, and consists in mixing cakes of neat cement, about 2 or 3 inches in diameter and $\frac{1}{2}$ inch thick, to a stiff plastic consistency, observing the time when they will bear a needle $\frac{1}{12}$ inch in diameter sustaining a weight of $\frac{1}{4}$ pound, and noting this as the beginning of setting ; then continuing the observations with a needle $\frac{1}{24}$ inch in diameter carrying a weight of one pound until the material is sufficiently firm to bear this when it may be called fully set. The committee call all those cements which set in one-half hour or less quick setting, those requiring more time slow setting. This method and nomenclature are commonly followed in this country.

In Germany and France the method commonly followed for accurate determination is that of the Vicat Needle. By this method a briquette of neat cement is made in a cylindrical brass or rubber mold, 10 cemtimeters in diameter and 4 centimeters high, placed upon a plate of glass or metal, the cement being mixed to a plastic condition as determined by the consistency test. The apparatus is so arranged that a weight of 300 grammes may be brought either upon a needle of 1 millimeter diameter or upon a cylindrical plunger of 1 centimeter diameter, and allowed to settle into the cement, the depth of penetration being shown by a scale along which the weight slides.

As soon as the mold is filled with the mortar, it is placed in the apparatus, and the plunger, sustaining the 300 grammes, is brought to the surface of the briquette and allowed to sink into it. If the plunger penetrates to a point 6 to 10 millimeters from the bottom, the mortar is of proper consistency for the test. The needle is then substituted for the plunger, and the time when the needle first refuses to sink entirely through the mortar is observed and noted as the beginning of setting ; the time when the needle first rests upon the briquette without penetrating it is considered the end of setting. This method gives slower results than the first one when the consistency is the same. It also gives more uniformity of result when conducted by different persons.

For ordinary practical purposes the common method is sufficiently accurate as all that is necessary to know is whether the cement sets quickly or slowly, but for experimental and comparative purposes the more elaborate method is valuable. The beginning of set is the point of most value to determine, as the cement in practice should be used before that point is reached, in order that it may not be disturbed after the stiffening has begun. It would seem that this point is better shown by the Vicat Needle, but in practical use the cement should be tested mixed as used in the work.

The time of setting is often roughly determined in practice, by making small cakes of mortar and observing when they will resist penetration under a light pressure of the thumb nail. This is a standard test in Germany.

The change of temperature during setting is also commonly observed in the European laboratories, and frequently in experimental work in this country. A rise in temperature, however, does not ordinarily occur except with quick cements, and does not seem to have any relation to the value of the material. When a rise in temperature occurs with a slow cement, it is said to indicate unsoundness, but for very slow cements a rise seldom occurs, even with flagrantly unsound material, which is appreciable upon a thermometer reading to one-fifth degree Fahrenheit.

Time of setting is usually measured in the air at about 60° or 70° Fahr. for purposes of comparison, but in case the material is to be placed under water before setting, it should be tested under water. The effect of the circumstances of use upon the activity of the material should always be tried when the conditions are unusual.

ART 13. TESTING THE TENSILE STRENGTH.

The tensile test is commonly used for the purpose of determining the strength of the cement mortar, because it can be more readily and uniformly applied than any other, and seems, coupled with other tests, to give a fair indication of the value of the material.

The proper conduct of a tensile test is a matter requiring care and experience. There are many points connected with the circumstances and manipulation of the test, which have an important bearing upon the result ; these are, the method of mixing and moulding the mortar, the form of the briquette, the amount and temperature of the water used in mixing, the temperature of the air at time of mixing, the temperature at which the briquette is kept during setting and hardening, and the rate and manner of applying the stress.

Temperature.—In standard tests it is customary to adopt a nearly constant temperature of 60°–65° Fahr. for the air of the laboratory during the making and setting of the briquettes, and about the same, or a slightly less temperature for the water used in mixing, and that in which the mortar is submerged during hardening. The effects of variations of temperature have been noted in Arts. 5 and 6.

Methods of Making Briquettes —The wide differences frequently observed in the results of different experimenters are, without doubt, mainly due to personal differences in making the briquettes. These differences occur not only in the work of novices, but in that of skilled operators, who, while usually able to maintain practical uniformity in their own work, disagree in results with each other when experimenting upon the same material and apparently using the same methods.

There are two methods in common use for making briquettes : the method recommended by the committee of the American Soicety of Civil Engineers, which is now commonly followed in this country, and to some extent in Europe, and the method given by the Association of German Cement Makers, which is more commonly employed in Europe.

The American Method as recommended by the committee is as follows : " The proportions of cement, sand and water should be carefully determined by weight, the sand and cement mixed dry and the water added all at once. The mixing must be rapid and thorough, and the mortar, which should be stiff and plastic, should be firmly pressed into the molds with a trowel, without ramming, and struck off level ; the molds in each instance while being charged and manipulated to be laid directly on glass, slate or some other non-absorbent material.

The molding must be completed before incipient setting begins. As soon as the briquettes are hard enough to bear it, they should be taken from the molds and be kept covered with a damp cloth until they are immersed. For the sake of uniformity, the briquettes, both of neat cement and those containing sand, should be immersed in water at the end of 24 hours, except in the case of one-day tests."

" The proportion of water required varies with the fineness, age or other conditions of the cement, and the temperature of the air, but is approximately as follows :

For briquettes of neat cement : Portland about 25%, Natural about 30%.

For briquettess of 1 part cement, 1 part sand : about 15% of total weight of sand and cement.

For briquettes of 1 part cement, 3 parts sand : about 12% of total weight of sand and cement.

The object is to produce the plasticity of rather stiff plasterer's mortar.''

By the German method the mortar is mixed more dry than in the above and the mold is filled heaped with it ; it is then rammed into place and pounded until the mortar grows elastic and the water flushes to the surface, after which the briquette is struck off level, and, as soon as it is hard enough, taken from the mold and treated as in the other case.

The French standard specifications require the mortar to be plastic and placed in the mold without ramming, but the side of the mold may be lightly tapped with the trowel to disengage the air bubbles that may remain in the mortar. This tapping of the mold is quite efficient in settling the mortar into place, and tends to give uniformity to the briquettes.

There are two points to be especially noted in making briquettes by hand : first, the mortar must be very thoroughly worked in mixing, both the French and German rules require that it shall be briskly mixed for five minutes, sufficient mortar being prepared at once for 5 or 6 briquettes; second, the air bubbles must be well worked out of the mortar in filling the molds. The neglect of these precautions causes much of the irregularity which commonly exists in the work of inexperienced operators. With more experienced men there exist differences in the amount of working, the pressure given in placing in the molds and the quantity of water used, which cause wide variations in results.

Mechanical Appliances for Making Briquettes.— In order to reduce the effect of the personality of the operator in making tensile tests of cement, various appliances for mixing and molding briquettes by machinery have been tried.

For mixing, an apparatus arranged to shake the materials rapidly up and down, on the principle of the ordinary milk shake, has been applied in a number of places, but usually without satisfactory results.

The mixing apparatus of Mr. Faija, with which good results are reported to have been obtained, consists of a cylindrical pan, in which a mixer, formed of four blades, revolves both on its own axis and about that of the pan. The writer has had good success in the use of a very similar apparatus, consisting of a closed brass cylinder, in which the mixer, composed of vertical rods held by a horizontal arm, revolves about the axis of the cylinder and also about the middle point of the arm. By the use of such an apparatus the mortar may be thoroughly mixed much more expeditiously than by hand, and with greater uniformity.

For molding the briquettes, the apparatus which has been most frequently applied is the Bohmé hammer, which consists of an arrangement by which 150 blows are struck by a hammer of 2 kilograms weight upon a plunger, sliding in a guide mold, placed over the mold in which the briquette is to be formed. A high degree of density is thus produced in the briquette, and the air is thoroughly expelled. More regular results are thus obtained, depending much less upon the personality of the operator, than by the ordinary method. The objection to the use of this method is the slow and tedious nature of the work.

A more satisfactory method of molding is by the use of a single application of a direct steady pressure. An apparatus for this purpose devised by Professor Jamieson of the University of Iowa has given satisfactory results, and has been introduced in a number of places. In this apparatus, appliances are also provided for the rapid feeding of the mortar to the mold and the immediate removal of the briquette from the mold.

It has been found by the writer that a pressure

of about 500 lbs upon the surface of the briquette
is sufficient to produce a compact and homogeneous briquette, and a crude appliance, consisting
of a lever arranged to bring a pressure upon the
mortar in the mold by means of a weight suspended at the end of the lever, has been found to
increase both the rapidity and the regularity of
the work, and especially to diminish the variations in results obtained by different men.

Greater uniformity in tensile tests of cement is
highly desirable and it seems possible to reach it
only by the application of automatic appliances
in making the briquettes. If a standard pressure
could be agreed upon, a simple and inexpensive
apparatus for molding briquettes could be readily
applied anywhere, and, coupled with some form
of mechanical mixer, would do much toward cor-
recting the irregularities that now exist.

Quantity of water used in mixing.—The rules
recommended by the committee of the American
Society of Civil Engineers require that the mortar used in making briquettes should be stiff and
plastic. The German rules, under which the
molding is done by pounding the mortar in the
molds, require that the mortar should be mixed
quite dry. In each case the water used depends
largely upon what idea the man doing the work
may have regarding what is meant by the terms
used in describing the process, and in practice a

very considerable variation will be found in this regard in the work of different men.

The French rules for standard tests, which are very similar in the method of making briquettes to those recommended by the committee of the American Society of Civil Engineers, give the following methods of determining if the mortar be of proper consistency :

1st. The consistency of the mortar should not change sensibly if the mixing be continued three minutes after the expiration of the required five minutes.

2nd. If a small quantity of the mortar be taken up on the trowel and allowed to fall upon the mixing slab from a height of 50 centimeters, it should be detached from the trowel without leaving any small particles adhering, and, after falling, should approximately retain its form without cracking.

3rd. A small quantity taken in the hand and patted into a round form, until water is brought to the surface, should not stick to the hand, and, when allowed to fall from a height of one-half meter, the ball should retain its rounded form without showing any cracks.

To meet these requirements leaves but a narrow limit within which the consistency may vary. If a slightly too small quantity of water be used, the mortar would crack upon falling. If the quantity be very slightly too great, the mortar will continue to soften upon further working, will be sticky, and will lose its form upon falling.

When the briquettes are molded by a machine, the quantity of water will necessarily be less than in hand work, and when using pressure the quantity may be regulated by making it all that the cement will take without having it squeezed out under the pressure. This will leave the briquette sufficiently firm to be immediately removed from the mold without injury.

Form of briquette.— Many forms of briquettes have been tried, but at the present time there are but two in common use : the one recommended by the committee of the American Society of Civil Engineers, which was originally used by Mr. Faija in England and is now standard in this country and commonly used in England ; the other is the one adopted by the Association of German Cement Makers and is the standard in France and Germany.

The principal difference in these forms is that in the American form the section diminishes gradually from the end to the middle, while in the German form the area is decreased suddenly by a circular notch at the middle. Comparative tests of briquettes of the two forms, having the same section, show that the English form will give higher results in nearly all cases than the German, the difference being usually 30 to 40 per cent. of the smaller. This may be accounted for by the fact, stated by Mr. Faija, that a sudden change of cross section is always an element of weakness.

In this country and in England, the standard minimum section of the tensile briquette is one square inch, in Germany and France it is five square centimeters.

The use of this small section is advantageous, both because it admits of using lighter apparatus in making the tests and because greater uniformity is attainable in preparing the small briquette. The strength obtained is greater per unit of area than would be had with larger specimens, and of course the strength by standard tests is much greater than can be developed by the material in actual use.

The size of the breaking section has an important effect upon resulting strength, the smaller the section, the higher the strength per unit of area.

M. Durand-Claye has shown that the strength varies with the perimeter of the section rather than its area, and that the interior may be removed leaving only a shell, without diminishing the strength.

Applying the Stress.—In order to produce uniform results in tensile tests, it is necessary that the stress shall be so applied as always to bring a direct tension upon the small section of the briquette, and also that the rate of application of the stress shall be uniformly the same. The rate of application commonly adopted is about 400 lbs. per minute. The machines in common use sometimes regulate this by causing the stress to be brought upon the briquette by the flow of a small stream of water or shot into a bucket suspended from the lever of the testing machine. This is highly satisfactory as giving uniformity of result, although there is a small impact due to the fall of the shot into the bucket, which may slightly affect the absolute measurement of the stress. In order that the stress upon the briquette shall be axial, care must be exercised in properly centering the briquette in the clip, and the form of the clip must be such that it shall not clamp or bind upon the head of the briquette, but may be free to adjust itself to an even bearing. The surface of contact between the briquette and clip must be large enough to prevent the material of the briquette being crushed at the point of contact, and as small as possible to permit of its more free self-adjustment. The suspension of the clips, as is usual, by conical bearings permits of their turning so as to transmit the stress in a right line between bearings.

Various devices have been proposed for the accurate centering of briquettes and to permit the more free adjustment of the clip to the direction of stress. In general, however, these do not seem necessary aud are of little practical value. The use of a rubber bearing between the clip and briquette, as devised by Mr. Cock, is said to produce satisfactory results, in facilitating the adjustment of the line of stress, and in the elimination of cross stresses and irregular breaks in the test pieces.

Sand Test.—Sand tests, although commonly recommended, are not very generally used in ordinary specifications, where reliance is usually placed upon the neat test, coupled with that for fineness, to indicate what the cement will do when mixed with sand. A tensile test with sand is, however, undoubtedly of the greatest value when properly conducted, as according more nearly with the conditions under which the cement is to be used than does the neat test.

In making briquettes for sand tests, it is of first importance that the cement and sand be very thoroughly mixed before the addition of the water.

The nature and degree of fineness of the sand has a very large influence upon the strength of the mortar. For standard tests in this country an artificial sand, made by crushing quartz, is used. The size of standard sand is such that it will pass through a sieve of 400 meshes per square inch, and be caught upon one of 900 meshes per square inch. Tests are also sometimes made with the sand which is to be used in the work, although this is rarely done.

Tensile Strength Required. — As has already been stated, the tensile strength developed by cement on a short time test is no necessary indication of the strength that may be attained by it during a longer period, unless the normal action of the particular material be known. That which is the strongest at first will not necessarily continue the strongest.

Mr. Faija recommends that the gain in strength between the 7 and 28 day periods be considered, rather than the absolute early strength, in determining the probable subsequent gain in strength. This is probably a better guide than the usual one, but it is not ordinarily practicable to require a test extending over a period of 28 days, and even were it possible, it would in many cases be misleading.

Professor Unwin gives a formula for the strength at any period, $y = a + b(x-1)^n$, in which y is the strength required at x weeks after mixing, a the strength at the end of one week, n a constant for the particular material to be determined by observation extending over considerable time, and b a constant to be determined from the strengths given by the sample at 1 and 4 weeks after mixing. Professor Unwin gives the value $n = \frac{1}{3}$ for Portland cement in general, and shows that the formula gives values according well with the results of tests in many instances. This formula, as will be readily seen, depends upon the assumption that for any two Portland cements the gains in strength at end of any period are to each other, as the gains between the 7 and 28 day tests, a proposition which for many Portland cements will scarcely hold, although approximately true for a considerable class of materials.

To make this method of practical use, it would be necessary to determine a formula for each kind or brand of cement.

It should be observed that some cements which quite closely follow the curve indicated by the formula, early reach their full strength, and make a quite abrupt break at the point which seems to mark the completion of the process of hardening, thus necessitating the use of an upper limit to the value of x, varying for different material.

Whatever may be the rate of subsequent hardening, the early tensile strength, when dealing with a material whose characteristics are known, is, without doubt, a very efficient help in the estimation of the value of a sample.

The strengths commonly required by specifications in this country are based upon the recommendations of the American Society of Civil Engineers, which are as follows :

"*American Natural Cement, Neat :*

1 day, 1 hour or until set in air, the rest of the 24 hours in water, from 40 to 80 pounds.

1 week, 1 day in air, 6 days in water, from 60 to 100 pounds.

1 month, 1 day in air, 27 days in water, from 100 to 150 pounds.

1 year, 1 day in air, remainder in water, from 300 to 400 pounds.

American and Foreign Portland Cements, Neat :

1 day, 1 hour or until set in air, the rest of the 24 hours in water, from 100 to 140 pounds.

1 week, 1 day in air, 6 days in water, from 250 to 550 pounds.

1 month, 1 day in air, 27 days in water, from 350 to 700 pounds.

1 year, 1 day in air, remainder in water, from 450 to 800 pounds.

American Natural Cements, 1 part Cement to 1 part of Sand :

1 week, 1 day in air, 6 days in water, from 30 to 50 pounds.

1 month, 1 day in air, 27 days in water, from 50 to 80 pounds.

1 year, 1 day in air, remainder in water, from 200 to 300 pounds.

American and Foreign Portland Cements, 1 part of Cement to 3 parts of Sand:

1 week, 1 day in air, 6 days in water, from 80 to 125 pounds.

1 month, 1 day in air, 27 days in water, from 100 to 250 pounds.

1 year, 1 day in air, remainder in water, from 200 to 350 pounds.''

At least the minimum values here given for 1 and 7 days are usually required in ordinary specifications. These values, however, need modification according to the kind of cement used, especially with the natural cements, which vary so widely in character. The requirements for each cement should depend upon what is known of it. Thus, natural cements from the Hudson, from the Potomac or from the Ohio, would need quite different specifications to insure good quality in each case.

The specifications, especially on large works where permanent laboratories are maintained, require modifications also according to the practice of the laboratories.

The results of tests in these laboratories is usually to give a higher strength for the same material than would be obtained on an ordinary outside test, especially by a comparatively inexperienced man. Lack of skill in conducting the test always tells against the material tested, while the extraordinarily high values, given out as obtained for some cements by certain of these fixed laboratories, are probably due more to skillful manipulation of the test than to differences in the material.

ART. 14. TESTS FOR SOUNDNESS.

Soundness is the most important quality of a cement, as it means the power of the cement to resist the disintegrating influences of the atmosphere or water in which it may be placed. Unsoundness in cement may vary greatly in degree, and show itself quite differently in different material. Cements in which the unsoundness is very pronounced are apt to become distorted and cracked after a few days, when small cakes are placed in water. Those in which the disintegrating action is slower may not show any visible change of form, but after weeks or months, even, may gradually lose coherence and soften until entirely disintegrated.

The method in common use for testing unsoundness is to make small cakes or pats of neat cement, usually about 3 or 4 inches in diameter and ½ inch thick, upon a plate of glass, and keep them in air or water for a few days, carefully watching them to see if they show any signs of distortion or surface cracks, which may indicate a tendency to disintegration.

The German standard specifications require that the cakes for this test shall be 1.5 centimeters thick at the center and have thin edges. These cakes are placed under water 24 hours after they are made, or at least not until they are firmly set, and observations are continued over a period of 28 days, when, if no crack or distortions appear, the cement is considered sound.

The method recommended by the committee of the American Society of Civil Engineers is to make two cakes or pats as for the German tests and observe them as follows :

"One of these cakes, when hard enough, should be put in water and examined from day to day to see if it becomes contorted, or if cracks show themselves at the edges, such contortions or cracks indicating that the cement is unfit for use at that time. In some cases the tendency to crack, if due to free lime, will disappear with age. The remaining cake should be kept in the air and its color observed, which for a good cement should be uniform throughout, yellowish blotches indicating a poor quality ; the Portland cements being of a bluish gray and the natural cements being light or dark, according to the character of the rock of which they are made. The color of the cements when left in the air indicates the quality much better than when they are put in water."

The color test above given is not considered to be of much value, as unsound cements are very commonly of good color.

The time during which these observations shall continue is not specified in these rules, but in practice they are not usually carried over more than from two days to a week before acceptance of the material.

It is important in testing soundness in this manner that the tests should be continued for as long a period as possible, and many cases of unsoundness will not be discovered even with a 28 day test. Cases have been observed in which mortar, in the form of 2 inch cubes, has completely disintegrated within two years, where incipient checking was not observable for three months in a small cake test. The most common and dangerous cases of unsoundness are probably discovered by the ordinary tests. It may be observed, however, that the fact, that cases of disintegrating mortar are not oftener observed in large constructions, is probably due more to the general good quality of the cement supplied by the best makers, and to the frequent stability of work regardless of the nature of the mortar, than to the efficiency of the test for soundness.

The quantity of water to be used in mixing cakes for these tests is about the same as that used for tensile tests, although a variation in the quantity does not seem to appreciably affect the result. Care should be taken in making these tests, that the cakes be kept in moist air during the setting and previous to immersion, in order that they may be free from drying cracks, which would not indicate any imperfection in the material.

ART. 15. ACCELERATED TESTS FOR SOUNDNESS.

The fact, that many cases of unsoundness in cement are not discoverable by the ordinary short time tests, is well known, and consequently several tests, intended to show more conclusively the value of the cement, have been proposed.

Most of these tests are based upon the idea of the advancement of the process of disintegration by the action of heat, and some of them have proven satisfaotory in use, although none of them have been extensively used in practice.

Hot tests were first suggested by Dr. Michaelis, who proposed to use heat for the advancement of hardening of the cement, claiming that cements kept in hot water would in a short time gain the full strength to be attained during a long time in cold water. This, while true of a certain class of cements, proved to be untrue of a large number of others of somewhat different composition. Subsequently Professor Le Chatelier proposed to modify the test, by advancing the idea that the gain in strength in hot water over that in cold water was an indication of the soundness of the cement, and suggesting the testing of briquettes of 1 to 3 mortar kept hot and cold, and accepting as sound that in which the strength of those kept hot is as great or greater than that of those kept cold, at the end of a few days.

Of this it may be said, as of the first proposition, that there are many cases in which it is untrue, some flagrantly unsound cements gaining strength very rapidly in hot as compared with what they will attain in cold water.

A few of the tests now proposed and used in different places are given below.

Kiln Test. This test, originaied by Dr. Bohmé, is included in the standard German specifications for cement which is to be used in the air. Under those specifications, cement to be used under water is also subjected to this test, but its result in this case is not considered decisive, the conclusive result being that of the 28 day cold water test, as given in Art. 14.

To make the kiln test, cakes of neat cement, made as for the ordinary cold test, after 24 hours in moist air, are placed in a drying oven and exposed to a temperature of 110° to 120° centigrade for at least an hour or until no more water escapes. If after this treatment the cakes show no edge cracks, the cement is to be considered sound.   In some cases this test is prolonged to 3 or 4 hours, and sometimes the heat is applied gradually.

This test is considered of value in Europe for use with cements to be used in air.   It has never been used in this country to any extent.   Cement to be used in water should be subjected to a wet test.

Steam and Hot Water Test.   This test consists in subjecting cakes of cement, prepared in the ordinary manner, to the action of steam for 3 or 4 hours, then immersing in hot water for the remainder of 24 hours, and examining for cracks and distortions.

Mr. Faija, by whom this test was devised, uses it in his specifications for cement in England. Mr. Faija describes his method of conducting the test as follows.

"Briefly, it is a vessel containing water, the water being maintained at an even temperature of about 110° to 115° Fahr.; there is a cover to the vessel, so that above the water there is a moist atmosphere which has a temperature of about 100° Fahr.   The manner of carrying out the test is by making a pat, in the manner already described, on a small piece of glass ; immediately the pat is gauged it is placed on a rack in the upper part of the vessel and is there acted upon by the warm vapor rising from the hot water, when the pat is set quite hard it is taken off the rack and put bodily into the water, which, as has been already stated, is maintained at a temperature of 110° to 115° Fahr., and in the course of 24 hours it is taken out and examined, and if found then to be quite hard and firmly attached to the glass, the cement may at once be pronounced sound and perfectly safe to use ; if, however, the pat has come off the glass and shows cracks or friability on the edges, or is much curved on the under side, it may at once be decided that the cement in its present condition is not fit for use.''

Mr. Faija prefers the temperature given above, · but other experimenters have seemed to get better results using a higher one. Prof. Tetmajer obtained fairly good results with a temperature just below the boiling point, about 200° Fahr , and subjected the cakes to the action of steam 4 hours, and hot water 20 hours, placing the cakes in the steam as soon as mixed.

Mr. Maclay has modified this method of testing, and introduced it into the specifications of the Department of Docks of New York City. Four pats or cakes of cement made in the usual manner are used by Mr. Maclay for his tests, the conduct of which he describes as follows.

'' One of these pats is placed in a steam bath,

temperature 195° to 200° Fahr., as soon as it is made. The second pat is placed in the same steam bath as soon as it is set hard, and can bear the 1 pound wire. The third pat is placed in the steam bath after double the interval has elapsed that it took the pats to set hard, counting from the time of gauging. The fourth pat is placed in the steam bath at the end of 24 hours.

"The first four pats are each kept in the steam bath 3 hours, then immersed in water of a temperature of about 200° Fahr. for 21 hours each, when they are taken out and examined. To pass this test perfectly, all four pats, after being 21 hours in hot water, should upon examination show no swelling, cracks nor distortions, and should adhere to the glass plates. The latter requirements, while it obtains with some cements nearly free from uncombined lime, is not insisted upon, the cracking, swelling and distortion of the pats being much the more important features of this test."

When only the first pat fails Mr. Maclay does not reject the cement but allows it the advantage of being set before being submitted to the steam. This lessens the severity of the test, and is a matter of judgment as to the degree of unsoundness that may be allowable.

Mr. Maclay also subjects those samples which fail upon this test to a second one before rejecting them, by testing the tensile strengths of briquettes kept in hot water and comparing them with those kept cold. If the hot strength is greater than that cold, he deems the cement normal in composition but perhaps underburned. The tests are made upon briquettes 2, 3, 4, and 7 days old, of 1 to 2 mortar. This is practically the method first suggested by Prof. Le Chatelier, already alluded to, and its use in this manner is recommended by M. Candlot, who states that cements of proper composition, slightly underburned, and capable of giving good results in use, may fail on the hot cake test, but will give good results in the hot strength test, when in a mortar containing sand.

The wisdom of thus qualifying the results of the steam and hot water test seems very questionable. As stated, at the beginning of this article, the action of heat to promote the hardening of mortar varies greatly with cement of slightly different compositions, and some of the worst of unsound cements show most satisfactory strengths in hot water.

Boiling Test.—This test consists in mixing cakes in the usual manner, placing them at once in cold water, raising the temperature of the water to boiling in about an hour, continuing boiling for three hours, and then examining for checking and softening. Its use is recommended by Prof. Tetmajer as the result of an extended series of experiments, including the use of the other hot tests, and observations of the material tested over long time under normal conditions.

This test is the most severe of those proposed, and may, as is sometimes claimed, reject certain underburned cements of good composition, but, in general, there seems to be no difficulty in the meeting of its requirements upon the part of good cements, either Portland or natural, although it is questionable whether certain light burned natural cements of the magnesian variety should be subjected to it.

If the cement be allowed to set before putting the cakes in the water, this test becomes practically the same as the steam and hot water test.

Professor Tetmajer recommends for this, and in fact for all pat tests, that the cakes shall not be made with thin edges. His method of making the pats is to roll a ball of the cement mortar, and flatten the ball to the required thickness. The mortar must be of such consistency as that it shall not crack in flattening, and shall not run at the edges. For the hot tests this method seems desirable, but in the slower cold tests still longer time would be required to obtain results than by the ordinary method.

Chloride of Calcium Test. This test is suggested by M. Candlot, and is designed to detect the presence of free lime or sulphate of lime in appreciable quantities.

The writer has found it to give true indications in a number of cases, including some unsound magnesian cements. It consists in mixing the mortar for the cakes, with a solution of 40 grammes chloride of calcium to 1 litre of water, allowing them to set, immersing them in the same solution for 24 hours, and then examining them for checking and softening as in the other tests.

There has been much discussion of late regarding these accelerated tests, and considerable opposition has been developed to their use in specifications, although in certain cases they have been so used. It has been definitely shown that, in general, certain of these tests do detect unsoundness in cement, where it can not be detected by the ordinary method. It has also been shown that good cements will usually pass them. It is possible that for different makes of cement there would be a variation in results for these, as there is for the other tests which are applied, but the reasonable presumption is against the soundness of any cement that fails upon nearly any of these tests when properly made.

Further experiments are desirable to determine the actual connection between the results of tests, and the action of the material during a long time under normal conditions.

When the action of these tests upon the different cements is more fully known, the tests may

be adapted to the material at hand so as to attain
the best results.   Until that time, however, it is
reasonable, upon all important work, to apply
such tests as will insure the good quality of the
material used, even at the risk of rejecting other
good material.

ART. 16.   CHEMICAL ANALYSIS.

Chemical tests are not commonly made for the
purpose ˚of determining the quality of cement,
and are only of limited value for that purpose,
in so far as the user is concerned.   The value of
cement depends not only upon its being composed of the proper relative quantities of the different ingredients, but also upon the state of combination of those ingredients, which in turn depends largely upon the care used in manufactur-
ing the cement.

The soundness of the cement cannot in general
be shown by analysis unless it contains too great
quantities of substances which are known to be
injurious, as for instance, a considerable percentage of sulphuric acid, or of magnesia, in Portland cement.   The existence of free lime can not
be shown by analysis, except as it may be inferred from a knowledge of the normal hydraulic
index of the material.

Under the French standard specifications, any
Portland cement is rejected which contains more

than 1% of sulphuric acid, or sulphides in appreciable quantity, while those with more than 4% of oxide of iron, or with a hydraulic index less than $\frac{44}{100}$, are regarded with suspicion. Similar requirements are imposed in some other European countries.

M. Candlot states that a chemical analysis may be useful in showing the adulteration of cement, sometimes practiced in Europe. Upon sifting the cement and separately analysing the coarse and fine portions, an unadulterated cement should show practically identical results for the two analyses. He also states that blast furnace slag, which is a common adulteration in Portland cement, may sometimes be discovered by the odor of sulphuretted hydrogen upon treating it with hydrocloric acid.

ART. 17. COMPRESSIVE TESTS.

The compressive strength of cement mortar is very much greater than its tensile or adhesive strength, and as it does not seem to give any better indication of value, while much more difficult of determination than the tensile strength, it is not usually employed as a test of quality. The compressive strength of mortar is commonly stated to be about 10 times its tensile strength although there is of course a considerable variation in the actual ratio.

In making compressive tests, cubes of 2 inch sides are generally used, these are moulded and treated in the same manner as the briquettes for tensile tests, and in breaking are commonly placed between the heads of the testing machine, with a thin layer of plaster of paris between the plate of the machine and the surface of the briquette, to bring it to an even bearing, and distribute the pressure uniformly.

The strength obtained upon a compressive test will vary with the size of the specimen used, the largest block giving the highest strength, and also as in the tensile test with the method of preparing the specimen. In Europe, standard test pieces for compressive tests are always moulded by the use of the hammer.

It may be noted that the compressive test differs from that for tension, in that the strength of the material of the whole block must be overcome to produce rupture, instead of that of the surface only, and that the compressive resistance in practice where the mortar is used in larger masses, will probably be greater than that of the test pieces.

Compressive tests are sometimes made, and are of great value, for the purpose of determining the strength actually developed in the work, under various contingencies of use.

ART. 18. ADHESIVE TESTS.

Adhesive tests are not commonly employed in determining the value of cement, because of the uncertain nature of the test, and the difficulty of so conducting it as to make it a reliable indication of value. Adhesive power is, of course, a very important characteristic of a cement, but an indication of this is obtained when the sand test is used, or when the neat tensile strength is coupled with a test for fineness.

It is to be observed that the adhesive strength is not necessarily proportional to that of cohesion, even when the fineness is the same, and that different varieties of cement may possess the property of adhesion in quite different degrees. The sand test, however, calls into play, to a certain extent, the adhesive power, and is at least a partial measure of adhesive strength.

Adhesive strength is developed much more stowly than cohesive, and the difference between the two, while very considerable on short time tests, may be gradually lessened with time. This may be seen illustrated in the fact that a cement which, when gauged neat, attains its full strength in a few weeks, may, when mixed with sand, continue to gain in strength for a year, and finally develop as much strengih as in the first case.

Experiments for the purpose of determining the adhesion of mortar to various substances are very desirable, in order to extend knowledge of the material in this most important, but little known, property.

The best method of conducting this test is probably to make briquettes, of which one-half shall be of cement of the ordinary form for tension, and the other half a piece of stone, glass or whatever surface is to be used, of the same section as the mold, at its middle, and arranged so that it may be caught in the clips of the testing machine at the other end. This may be accomplished by filling out with cement or plaster if necessary, or a special clamp may be used in place of the clip for catching a rectangular block at one end of the briquette, which must be left free to adjust itself to an axial stress.

ART . 19. MICROSCOPIC TESTS.

Tests for cement by miscroscopic examination have been proposed, and some observations made for the purpose of determining whether any idea of the quality of the cement could be obtained from such examination, with varying results. While it is unlikely that such a test will come into general use for determinations of value, it is quite probable that much may thus be learned concerning the nature and action of the material.

There are two methods by which such work may be carried out ; first, by cutting sections of unground cement rock, or of briquettes made of the cement, and examining its constitution in the ordinary method for rock ; and second, by examining the cement powder under the microscope, and noting the character of the grains of which it is composed.

With cements of the Portland class, it has been observed that the active portion of the cement is composed of grains of angular form and metallic lustre, and that the portions having an earthy appearance are probably inert. It has also been found that the color of the grains seem to bear some relation to their value in the material, although this has not been investigated sufficiently to state any general deductions.

Professor Le Chatelier by his study of sections of unground Portland cement rock has added very greatly to the knowledge of the constitution of Portland cement ; much however remains to be done in this direction.

ART. 20. ABRASION TESTS.

In Germany tests of the resistance of cement blocks to abrasion are frequently employed, especially where the material is to be subjected to wear in use, as in walks.

For this purpose the apparatus of Prof. Bauschinger is commonly employed. This apparatus consists essentially of a cast iron rotating disk upon which the specimen is held, with constant pressure, by a weight at the end of a lever. A certain amount of sand is used to assist the grinding action, and after a given number of turns the loss of weight of the specimen is determined. Thus the comparative value of various cements to resist wear, as well as of various mixtures of cement and sand are determined.

It has been found that mortars containing small proportions of sand resist wear better than those of neat cement.

ART. 21. AIR SLAKING.

Sometimes fresh cement, when first opened after being shipped, will, if tested, show an abnormally rapid rate of setting, and subsequently harden very slowly, so that on short time tests very low tensile strength will be given. If, however, this cement be exposed to the air for a few days, it may resume its natural rate of setting, and attain proper strength upon the tests. In some laboratories it is customary to thus expose cement to the air a short time before testing, and this process is termed *air slaking*.

The propriety of air slacking in testing cement is questioned by some engineers, upon the ground that the cement to be used in the work will not be treated in the same manner. In England, it is customary to give such exposure to all cement to be used upon important work for at least ten days, but in this country the cement is commonly used just as received from the manufacturer.

The general practice seems to be in favor of air slaking the cement in testing it, and it seems probable that a cement capable of regaining its normal condition in a few days will not endanger the work, even if used at once, but it would doubtless be better in using such cement, to air slake the whole of it before using.

In many cases the strength after three or six months will be as great, when it is mixed before, as when after air-slaking, although the difference of strength on a test extending over a few days is very considerable.

If the cement blows or shows unsoundness on the first test, the propriety of using it in the work, without first exposing it to the air, is more doubtful, even though this point be also regained on the second test,

CHAPTER. III.

ART. 22.   SAND FOR MORTAR.

As hydraulic cement is nearly always mixed with certain proportions of sand, when used in construction, the nature and quantity of sand used, and the method of manipulating the materials in forming the mortar have an effect nearly as important upon the final strength of the work as the quality of cement itself.

In testing cement, as has been stated in art 13. an artificial sand, made by crushing quartz, is commonly employed. This sand may be had quite uniform in quality. In the execution of work, however, natural sand from the locality must generally be used ; this will vary widely in its nature, and should always be carefully considered upon any important work where the development of strength and lasting qualities in the mortar is of importance.

A sand for use in mortar should be as clean and free from loam, mud or organic matter as possible. A small admixture of pure clay may not be objectionable, and has been shown in some instances not to decrease the strength, when present to an extent not exceeding ten per cent. of the sand. But, in general, the presence of any foreign matter in the sand is to be avoided, and M. Alexandre has shown that clay, in mortar to be used in sea water, may be an element of danger, acting like unsound cement to cause disintegration.

The sand should also be as sharp as possible; if it be composed of angular grains, it will compact much closer and make a much stronger mortar, when used with the same proportion of cement, than if it be composed of rounded grains.

Uniformity of size of grain is also desirable when the mortar contains a considerable proportion of sand.

Coarse sand is preferable to that which is very fine, giving better strength to the mortar, especially in the case of mortar rich in cement. Fine sand may, however, be desirable when an impervious mortar is the object.

In using a quick setting cement the dryness of the sand is a matter of importance, as, if the sand be damp, when the mixture of sand and cement is made, sufficient moisture may be given off to the cement to induce a partial setting previous to the addition of the water. With slow setting cement this is of less consequence.

The proportion of sand to cement to be used in any case, depends upon the nature of the work and the necessity for the development of strength or imperviousness in the mortar. The relative quantities of sand and cement should also depend upon the nature of the sand, although this element is not usually considered.

The proportions most commonly used in ordinary work are, for natural cements, one part of cement to one part of sand, or in some cases, one part of cement to two parts of sand, and for Portland cement, one part of cement, to three parts of sand. If the proportions of the mixture were regulated by the value of the sand, the interests of economy might frequently require changes in proportions and would generally demand the use of the best sand obtainable A good sand mixed in a 1 to 3 mortar will frequently give better strength than a poorer sand mixed in the proportion of 1 to 2, and either mortar give equally good results in practice.

It is not, of course, practicable to use these materials with any certainty as to the absolute strength that is being attained in the work, but a test of the sand used, under the actual conditions of use, might often contribute largely to our knowledge of the result that is being produced. The best way to value the sand for use is by testing it in comparison with the standard testing sand, and many natural building sands will show results as to strength of mortar equal or superior to that sand.

ART. 23. WATER FOR MORTAR.

The quantity of water to be used in mixing
mortar can be determined only by experiment in
each case. It depends upon the nature of the
cement, upon that of the sand and of the water,
and upon the proportion of sand to cement.

Fine sand requires more water than coarse sand
to give the same consistency, and the mortar with
fine sand should be made a little more wet than
with coarse sand to give the best results in the
work. Dry sand will take more water than that
which is moist, and sand composed of porous
material more than that which is hard. As the
proportion of sand to cement is increased, proportion of water to cement should also increase,
but in a much less ratio. Less sea water than
fresh will be required to produce a given consistency.

The amount of water to be used in mixing
mortar for ordinary masonry is such that the mortar when thoroughly mixed shall have a stiff
plastic consistency.

It should not be a soft, semi-fluid mass. The
required consistency is described by M. Candlot[*]
as such that if a ball of mortar be formed in the
hand and allowed to fall through a small height,

---

[*] Ciment et Chaux Hydraulique, E. Candlot, Paris, 1891.

it should neither lose its form nor crack ; the ball should not be wet enough to stick to the hand.

The greatest cohesive strength will be given by mixing as dry as possible, while the adhesive strength will be greater in a wet mixture. The best results are obtained in practice by mixing the mortar with as little water as will admit of its proper manipulation and thoroughly wetting the surface to which it is to adhere.

In all cases the proper quantity of water should first be determined by experiment upon small quantities of the materials, and afterward, in preparing the mortar for use in the work, the required quantity should each time be added by measurement. The addition of the water little by little, or from a hose, should never be allowed.

ART. 24.   MIXING MORTAR.

In mixing cement mortar, the cement and sand are first thoroughly mixed dry, the water then added and the whole worked to a uniformly plastic condition.

The value of the mortar will depend upon the thoroughness of the operation ; the cement must be uniformly distributed through the sand during the dry mixing, and thoroughly working the mass after the addition of the water will greatly increase its strength.

In mixing by hand, by the ordinary method, a

platform or box is used ; the sand and cement are placed upon the platform in layers, with a layer of sand at bottom, and then turned and mixed with shovels until properly distributed through the mass. The material is then formed into a ring, or into a mound with a crater at the center, and all the water necessary added at once being placed in the center, after which the material is thrown up from the sides until the water is all taken up, and is then worked into a plastic condition.

In order to secure proper manipulation of the materials, on the part of the workmen, it is quite common to require that the whole mass shall be turned over a certain number of times with the shovels, both dry and wet.

The mixing should be quickly and energetically done, only such quantity being mixed at once as can be used before the initial set of the mortar takes place.

The cement should not be left in contact with the sand for any considerable time before being used, or a considerable quantity should not be mixed dry and left to stand until wanted, as the moisture, usually in the sand, will, to some extent, act upon the cement.

Upon large works, mechanical mixers are frequently employed with the advantage of at once lessening the labor of manipulating the material and insuring good work. There are a number of forms of mixers which do thorough and satisfactory work.

ART. 25.   CONCRETE.

Concrete is usually formed of a mixture of broken stone, or gravel, with sufficient cement mortar to bind the mass firmly together. The stone used should be as hard and durable as possible, and that of angular form and uniform size will give better results than if it be rounded and uneven. Angular forms give a greater surface for the adherence of the mortar in proportion to the volume, while leaving a less volume of interstices to be filled by the mortar. The amount of sand used should be such as will just fill the voids in the stone, while the quantity of cement will depend upon the strength necessary to develop for the particular work under consideration.

When the concrete is required to be water tight, the amount of cement must be sufficient to fill the interstices in the aggregate composed of the combined sand and stone.

The amount of sand necessary to fill the interstices in the stone may be determined by filling a measure with stone, as closely as possible, and then measuring the quantity of water which can be poured into the measure ; this will give the volume of sand required. If the proper quantity

of damp sand be added to the stone in the measure by shaking it down so as to fill the voids, the
volume of water which can then be put into the
measure will be the volume of cement necessary
to fill the voids in the aggregate.

The strength of the concrete will usually vary
nearly in proportion to the amount of cement
used in forming it. When a strong concrete is
desired, it should be obtained by increasing the
richness of the mortar in cement, not by increasing the proportion of mortar to large material
above the point where the sand fills the interstices
in that material. If the proportion of sand be
less than this, the resulting concrete will be porous and not thoroughly solidfied ; if it be greater,
the excess of sand will be an element of weakness in the concrete.

In the use of concrete in considerable masses,
the main body of the work is sometimes formed
of a very weak concrete, with a facing of stronger
watertight concrete to protect it. This weak concrete is frequently formed by omitting the sand
altogether, and simply coating the stone lightly
with neat cement mortar, causing the stones to adhere to each other, thus forming a mass sufficiently firm for foundations in many locations
when protected by a covering of richer concrete.
The voids in a mass of ordinary broken stone
vary from about $\frac{4}{10}$ to $\frac{5}{10}$ of the volume, depend-

ing upon uniformity of size. The proportions in common use for concrete of Portland cement vary from 1 part cement, 2 parts sand, and ·5 parts broken stone to 1 part cement, 4 parts sand and 8 or 10 parts broken stone or gravel. Usually the mortar is made somewhat richer when natural cement is to be used. The proportions, of course must vary with the character of the materials to be used, as well as that of the work to be done, and can only be properly determined by the exercise of good judgment in the light of experience.

In preparing concrete, the mortar is mixed in the usual manner, then the stone is spread over the top of the layer of mortar and thoroughly mixed with it by turning with shovels. The stone should be sprinkled sufficiently to wet its surface before being mixed with the mortar, in order to prevent the absorption of the water from the mortar, and to promote the adherence of the mortar to the stone.

The mortar for concrete should never, as is quite commonly done, be reduced to a fluid state ; not only will the mortar be weakened by so doing, but it cannot be properly mixed with the stone to form a homogeneous mass, as the cement will wash out of the mixture.

Mechanical mixers are frequently employed for preparing concrete, and are very useful in the saving of labor especially where considerable quantities are being used.

Concrete should always be used immediately after mixing, and should not be disturbed after the initial set of the cement. It will also be benefitted by being well rammed into place.

ART. 26. MIXTURES OF LIME AND CEMENT.

Common slaked lime is frequently mixed with Portland, or natural cement for the purpose of decreasing the cost of construction. In works to be exposed mainly to the air, experiment seems to indicate that a very considerable percentage of lime may sometimes be added without material loss of strength in the mortar.

For mortar to be used under water, the loss of strength is greater when lime is mixed with the cement, and the propriety of its use is more questionable.

Experiments in this matter have not been sufficiently extended to admit of any general deductions. The question of the advisability of such mixture in any case is mainly an economic one, and turns upon the determination of whether it be cheaper to form a certain volume of mortar of given strength by the use of the mixed lime and cement, or by the use of the cement alone with more sand.

The admixture of lime causes the cement to become slower setting, affecting the quick setting cements more strongly than the less active ones. In damp situations the durability of the mixture is also open to question.

In France, a small percentage of Portland ce- ment is sometimes added to hydraulic lime, with the effect, it is claimed, of considerably augment- ing the strength and also of accelerating the set- ting of the lime.

Mixtures of natural with Portland cements have frequently been used in this country, and seem, in general, to give a result which is a mean of the properties of the cements mixed. In all of these cases, in order to obtain good results the mixture must be very intimate.

ART. 27. FREEZING OF MORTAR.

Mortar of good Portland, or of many kinds of natural cement, is not injured in strength by freezing, even if it be frozen before it is set. The cement will not set while frozen, but, if allowed to thaw out, will afterward set.

The hardening of cement which has been frozen will be much more slow than if unfrozen, but it may ultimately gain the same strength.

Masonry constructed in freezing weather will frequently be injured by freezing, notwithstand- ing the fact that the cement itself shows no loss of strength due to freezing. The effect of frost coming upon the work before it is fully hardened is frequentiy to distort or cause unequal settlement in it, and sometimes repeated freezing and thawing gradually causes the mortar to force out and crack off, or perhaps disintegrate on the outside. The construction of cement masonry during freezing weather is therefore, generally, more or less hazardous, unless some means be taken to prevent the freezing action. Many instances may, however, be cited, where extreme cold has not injured work constructed, without such precaution, with Portland cement mortar, and it is claimed by many engineers that Portland cement may be used with impunity in freezing weather, but usually it is not placed in the work while a freezing temperature prevails. It is commonly agreed that most natural cements should not be used when a very low temperature is likely to reach the work in advance of its having attained good strength, and instances are numerous where work has been injured by the changing temperatures of winter weather, although it may have been constructed several weeks before being frozen.

Salt is very commonly used in cold weather to prevent the freezing of the mortar while it is soft. A strong solution, frequently a saturated one, is employed. The salt, by preventing the freezing of the water, prevents any distorting or disrupting action upon the work due to the change in volume of the mortar. The salt has, of course, no effect to prevent injury to the cement in any case in which a loss of strength would result from a low temperature without its use.

The use of salt in mortar considerably decreases the activity of the cement, and mortar will not usually set at freezing temperatures, even if salt be used to prevent freezing, or at least, the setting action at low temperatures is so slow as to be imperceptible during several days. Usually no injury will be done the mortar by standing in a soft condition at freezing temperatures as the volume will not change, it can not dry out, and when a sufficient temperature is reached it will set, but much more slowly than if it had not been exposed to the low temperature.

The decrease of early strength in cement mortar, which has been mixed with salt water, when exposed to a low temperature, is usually greater than that of mortar of the same cement mixed without the salt and frozen at the same temperature.

The effect of salt upon the strength of various kinds of cement is quite different. In nearly all, the strength of mortar kept in the air is increased by its use. When the mortar is kept in water, most cements will have an access of early strength from the use of salt, which will later be lost, the final strength being somewhat reduced. This is true of nearly all Portland cements Some natural cements suffer a material loss of strength when mixed with salt water, while others are entirely ruined by a low temperature with or without the admixture of salt. In general, however, the natural cements derive more benefit than Portlands from the use of salt. Care should always be taken to determine the action of salt and cold upon the particular cement before applying it in use.

Care should be taken in using salt, that after the mortar has been subjected to a freezing temperature it does not come into contact with water for a considerable time, as mortar contain-. ing salt, after it has warmed up and set, will frequently be softened and disintegrated by the action of water, unless sufficient time has elapsed to admit of its hardening sufficiently to resist such action.

Soda is sometimes employed to prevent the freezing of mortar, but its use has not become extensive.

Hot water should not be used in mixing mortar in freezing weather, as it not only decreases the strength of the mortar, but renders it more liable to injury from frost. Heating the stones or bricks in the construction of masonry in freezing weather may be beneficial, as serving to accelerate the setting and keep the cement from freezing while soft.

The injury done to mortar by freezing, however, is probably not usually due to freezing before setting, but to alternate thawing and freezing while the work is still fresh, and before hardening is sufficiently advanced to be capable of adequately resisting the disrupting forces. The effect of frost upon mortar which has set is similar to that upon stone or brick, and is due to the increase of volume of the water which freezes in the pores of the mortar. Its effect, therefore, depends both upon the porosity of the mortar and upon the strength it possesses to resist disruption. The more rapid acquisition of strength by the Portland cements may give them the advantage they usually possess in this regard.

ART. 28. POROSITY AND PERMEABILITY OF MORTARS.

The permeability of cement mortars varies with the quality of the cement and the circumstances of its use. Mortar of neat Portland cement may be made practically impermeable under a considerable head of water; that composed of cement and sand seems always more or less permeable, but when properly proportioned and mixed will eventually permit very little water to pass under small heads.

The permeability of mortar decreases rapidly with lts age ; for the first few days or weeks after mixing water passes quite freely through it, but as the hardening process approaches completion its power of resistance is, in this particular, greatly augmented.

Both the porosity and permeability are less for mortar rich in cement than for that in which the proportion of cement is small. Mortar mixed dry is penetrated more readily than that mixed to a plastic or semi-wet condition. The thoroughness of mixing and degree of compacting employed are, however, more important factors than the absolute quantity of water used in mixing.

Fine sand, according to the experiments of M. Alexander, renders the mortar more porous and less permeable than coarse sand. When the sand is of varying sizes, both the porosity and permeability may be low. In any case, to attain a reasonable resistance to penetration, it is necessary that the interstices in the sand be entirely filled with cement. Cleanliness of the sand, and its freedom from all foreign material, is of first importance in the preparation of impermeable mortar.

Masonry of ordinary brick or stone can only be made impervious by the application of a coating of some kind to its face. A plastering of neat cement or of rich mortar may frequently be used

for this purpose and coatings of asphaltum or coal tar have sometimes been successfully employed.

In concrete work where imperviousness is essential it is advisable, as with masonry, to coat the face of the concrete. In order that concrete may be made reasonably watertight, it is necessary that the quantity of cement mortar used in preparing it be sufficient to fill the voids in the large material employed, as well as, that the voids of the sand be completely filled with cement in making the mortar.

ART. 29.   EXPANSION AND CONTRACTION OF MORTAR.

In the use of large masses of masonry, or concrete, the change that is liable to occur in the volume of mortar may frequently become of importance, and it may be necessary to make provison by which change of dimension can take place without injury to the work.

The coefficient of expansion of neat cement mortar, under the action of heat, is, as already stated, approximately the came as that of iron, although there may be a considerable variation in some cases. For mortar containing sand the coefficient is less than for neat cement.

Cements differ considerably in their behavior during the continuance of the hardening process, as to the change that takes place in the volume of the mortar. Unsound cements are apt to swell and become distorted at the commencement of the process of disintegration, and, of course, any considerable change of this nature indicates the probable destruction of the mortar. Perfectly sound cement, although not altered in form, is usually changed somewhat in dimensions during hardening ; if the mortar be kept in dry air, a slight shrinkage takes place ; if under water, the mortar swells a little.

Professor Swain, in a series of experiments made at the Massachusetts Institute of Technology for a committee of the American Society of Civil Engineers, found that, for small blocks of mortar, the change was the same in all directions ; that for neat cements, the linear contraction in air varied from 0.14% to 0.32% for the first 12 weeks after mixing, and the linear expansion in water varied from 0.04% to 0.25%. When sand was used the change was less, giving a contraction in air of from 0.08% to 0.17% and an expansion in water of from 0.00% to 0.08%.

The rapidity of the change in volume varies also, to some extent, with the activity of the cement ; the conclusion being that a quick setting cement changes more in volume than a slow setting one.

Further experiment upon this point is desirable

in order that the action of the various classes of cements may be better understood.

ART. 30. EFFECT OF RETEMPERING MORTAR.

Masons very frequently mix mortar in considerable quantities, and, if the mass becomes stiffened, before being used, by the setting of the cement, add more water and work again to a soft or plastic condition. After the second tempering, the cement is much less active than at first and will remain for a longer time in a workable condition.

This practice is now very generally condemned by engineers and is not usually allowed in good engineering construction, although there is considerable dispute as to the injurious effect of retempering upon the mortar. M. Alexander, from a large series of experiments concerning this matter, concludes that no injury is usually done to the mortar by retempering it, provided sufficient water be added to make the material plastic at the second working. The hardening of mortar so treated is at first very slow, and it gives very low early strength, but it may subsequently (the tests extend over 3 years) gain as much strength as when gauged immediately upon mixing.

Other experimenters have seemed to show that in some cases injury is done to mortar by retempering, some cement even refusing to set the second time. In the light of our present knowledge, therefore, it seems advisable to mix only such quantity at once as may be used before the initial set of the cement, and to reject any material that may have become set before being placed in the work.

CHAPTER IV.

LITERATURE RELATING TO CEMENT.

ART. 31.   LIST OF PERIODICAL LITERATURE.

The following list of literature, relating to hydraulic cement, has been arranged for the purpose of aiding students in making special study of the subject. Only such papers have been included as seem to possess some definite value for purposes of research. The list is, for the most part, limited to works which may be found in the Cornell University Library, and is far from complete, but includes many of the more important recent contributions to the knowledge of the subject.

PAPERS IN ENGLISH.

1. ALEXANDRE, PAUL.— Porosity and Permeability of cement morters and their decomposition by sea water. *Engineering News, Jan. 10, 1891.*
2. ARNOLD, H.—Effect of sand upon the strength of Cement. *Eng. News, July 11, 1885.*
3. BAKER. I. O.—Economy in the composition of cement mortar. *Eng. News, March 10, 1888.*
4. BAMBER, H. K.— Portland Cement, its manufacture, use and testing. *Proc. Institution Civ. Eng., Vol. 107, p. 31.*
5. BECKWITH, ARTHUR.— The Composition of Ancient Cement and Rosendale Cement. *Trans. Am. Soc. C. E., Vol. 11, p. 171.* Also *Van Nostrand's Mag., Vol. 8, p. 205.*
6. BERNAYS, E. A.—Portland Cement Concrete. *Proc. Institution Civil Engineers, Vol. LXII, p. 87.*

7. BOSWELL, ST. GEORGE.—The Quebec Harbor Improvements. *Trans. Canadian Soc. C. E., Vol. 1, part 2, p. 77.*

8. BROWN, A. H.—Microscopic Tests for Cements. *Eng. News, Nov. 21, 1891.*

9. BRUNER, P. M.—Effect of low temperatures on Portland cement concrete. *Jour. Assoc. Eng. Soc., Vol. 7, p. 125.*

10. BURNETT, S. F.—Selection, Inspection and Use of Cements. *Jour. Assoc. Eng. Soc., Vol. 7, p. 258.* Also *R. R. Gazette, v. 20, p. 754.*

11. BUTLER, M. J.—The Manufacture of Natural Cements. *Trans. Canadian Soc. C. E., Vol. IV, p. 95.*

12. CAREY, A. E.—The testing of Portland Cement for Public Works. *Proc. Inst. Civil Eng., Vol. 107, p. 40.*

13. CHIBAS, E. J.—Cost of Concrete and Masonry. *Engineering Record, Apr. 11, 1891.*

14. CLARK, E. C.—Record of Tests of Cement made for Boston Drainage Works. *Trans. Am. Soc. C. E., Vol. XIV, p. 141.*

15. COCK, W. R.—Letters describing rubber bearing for clips. *Engineering News, Jan. 17, 1891, and Dec. 22, 1892.*

16. COLSON, CHARLES.—Experiments on the Portland Cement used in the Portsmouth Dockyard Extension Works. *Proc. Inst. C. E., Vol. XLI, p. 125.*

17. DE SMEDT, E. J.—New York Dock Department Cement Tests. *A letter in Eng. News, Dec. 5, 1891.*

18. DE SMEDT, E. J.—Chemical Tests for Cement. *Letters in Eng. News, Dec. 26, 1885, Jan. 23, and Feb. 13, 1886.*

19. DURAND-CLAYE and DEBRAY.—Permeability of Cement Mortar. (See paper No. 111.) *Jour. Franklin Inst., March, 1889 ;* also *Eng. Record. Nov. 23, 1889.*

20. ENGLER.—Cement, Hydraulic Lime, Roman Cement, Portland Cement. *Eng. News, Feb. 7 and Feb. 14, 1891.*

21. FAIJA, HENRY.—On the Mechanical Examination and Testing of Portland Cement. *Proc. Inst. C. E., Vol. 75, p. 213.*

22. FAIJA, HENRY.—Portland Cement. *Trans. Society of Engineers, June, 1885.*
23. FAIJA, HENRY.—Portland Cement Testing. *Trans. Am. Soc. C. E., Vol. 17, p. 218.*
24. FAIJA, HENRY.—On the Manufacture and Testing of Portland Cement. *Paper before Engineers' Congress, Chicago, 1893*
25. FERET, R.—Mortar for Sea Works. *Engineering, July 28, 1893.*
26. FRANCIS, J. B.—High Walls or Dams to Resist the Pressure of Water. *Trans. Am. Soc. C. E., Vol. 19, p. 147.*
27. FREEMAN, H. C.—Cement Works of the Utica Cement Co. *Trans. Am. Inst. Mining Eng., Vol. 13, p. 172.*
28. FRISWELL, R. J.—Manufacture of Slag Cement. *Eng. Record, Nov. 12, 1887.*
29. GARY, MAX.—The Testing of Portland Cement and the Development of the Cement Industry in Germany. *Paper before Engineers' Congress, Chicago, 1893.*
30. GRANT, JOHN.—Experiment upon the Strength of Portland Cement. *Proc. Inst. C. E., Vol. 32, p. 266.*
31. GRANT, JOHN.—Portland Cement, its Nature, Tests and Uses. *Proc. Inst. C. E., Vol. 62, p. 98.*
32. GRANT, WM. H.—Notes on Cement, Mortars and Concretes. *Trans. Am. Soc. C. E., Vol. 25, p. 259.*
33. HYDE and SMITH.—Permeability of Cement Mortar. *Jour. Franklin Inst., Sept., 1889.*
34. KINIPPLE, W. R.—Concrete Work Under Water. *Proc. Inst. C. E., Vol. 87, p. 65;* also abstract in *Eng. Record, Feb. 21, 1891.*
35. KUICHLING, E.—Cement Mortar for Public Works. *Eng. Record, March 24 and 31, Apr. 14 and 21, 1888.*
36. LARNED, W. F.—Mixing and Handling Concrete at Boston Water Works. *Eng. News, Dec. 24, 1887.*
37. LE CHATELIER, H.—The Composition of Cement Under the Microscope. (From paper 121.) *The Builder, Vol. 42, p. 701.*
38. LE CHATELIER, H.—Tests of Hydraulic Materials. *Paper before Engineers' Congress, Chicago, 1893.*

39. LESLIE, R. W.—Letter Concerning a New Form of Cement Specification. *Eng. News, Aug. 22, 1891.*
40. LOWCOCK, S. R.—Strength of Concrete Slabs. *Proc. Institution, C. E., Vol. 111, p. 352;* also *Eng. News, May 4, 1893.*
41. LUNDIE, JOHN.—Concrete. *Jour. Assoc. Eng. Soc., Vol. 6, p. 437.*
42. MACLAY, W. W.—Notes and Experiments on the Use and Testing of Portland Cement. *Trans. Am. Soc. C. E., Vol. VI, p. 311,* with discussion in *Vol. VII, p. 280.*
43. MACLAY, W. W.—Hot Tests for determining change of volume in Portland Cement. *Trans. Am. Soc. C. E., Vol. 27, p. 412.*
44. MANN, I. J.—The Adhesive Strength of Portland Cement. *Proc. Inst. Civ. Eng., Vol. 71, p. 412.* Also *Van Nostrand's Mag., Vol. 29, p. 233.*
45. MANN, I. J.—The Testing of Portland Cement. *Proc. Inst. Civ. Eng., Vol. 47, p. 248.*
46. MASSY, G. H. — Foundations of the St. Lawrence Bridge. *Trans. Canadian Soc. C. E., Vol. 1, p. 36.*
47. MESSENT, P. J.—Concrete in Sea Water. *London Engineering, Jan. 27, 1888.*
48. MICHAELIS.—The Manufacture and Use of Portland Cement. *Van Nostrand's Mag., Vol. 1, p. 746.*
49. MICHAELIS, W.—The behavior of Portland Cement in Sea Water. *Proc. Inst. Civ. Eng., Vol. 107, p. 371.*
50. MILLER, T. D.—The Louisville Cements. *Jour. Assoc. Eng. Soc., Vol. 5, p. 187.*
51. MURPHY, M.—Concrete as a substitute for Masonry in Bridge Work. *Trans. Canadian, Soc. C. E., Vol. 2, p. 79.*
52. MURPHY, M.—Bridge Substructure in Nova Scotia. *Paper before Engineers' Congress, Chicago, 1893.*
53. NEWKIRCH, FR.—Improved method of constructing Foundations under water by forcing cement into loose sand or gravel. *Paper before Engineers' Congress, Chicago, 1893.*
53a. NOBLE, ALFRED.—Effect of Freezing upon Mortar. *Trans. Am. Soc. C. E., Vol. 16, p. 79.*

54. NOBLE, ALFRED.—Experiments with appliances for Testing Cements. *Trans. Am. Soc. C. E.*, *Vol. 9, p. 186.*

55. NORTON, F. O.—American Natural Cements. *Trans. Am. Soc. C. E.*, *Vol. 9, p. 280.*

56. PARSONS, H. DE B.—The Influence of Sugar upon Cement. *Trans. Am. Soc. Mechanical Eng.*, *Vol. 9, p. 286.*

57. POWERS, M. I.—The Effect of Salt upon Cement Mortars. *Eng. News, Nov. 21, 1891.*

58. PRIME, F.—The Cement Works on the Lehigh. *Second Geol. Surv. of Penn'a, 1876, Vol. DD.*

59. RANSOME, F. — Improvements in Manufacture of Portland Cement. *The Builder, Sept. 17, 1887.*

60. REDGRAVE, G. R.—Slag Cement. *Proc. Inst. C. E.*, *Vol. CV, p. 215.* Abstract in *Eng. and Min. Jour.*, *May 24, 1890.*

61. RUSSELL, S. BENT.—Neat Test vs. Sand Tests for Portland Cements. *Trans. Am, Soc. C. E.*, *Vol. 25, p. 295.*

62. RUSSELL, S. B.—The Cement Laboratory of the St. Louis Water Works Extension. *Eng. News, Jan. 3, 1891.*

63. SABIN, L. C.—Variation in Cement Testing Sieves. *Eng. News, June 30, 1892.*

64. SCHERMERHORN. — Concrete Breakwaters. *Eng. News, Jan. 31, 1891.* *Eng. Record, May 16, 1891.*

65. SCOTT AND REDGRAVE.—The Manufacture and Testing of Portland Cement. *Proc. Inst. C. E.*, *Vol. 62, p. 67.*

66. SLATER, JOHN.—Concrete. *The Builder, March 20, 1882.*

67. SMITH, W.—Influence of Sea Water on Portland Cement. *Proc. Inst. Civ. Eng.*, *Vol. 107, p. 73.*

68. SONDERICKER, J.—Investigation as to how to Test the Strength of Cements. *Jour. Assoc. Eng. Soc.*, *Vol. 7, p. 207.*

69. SPALDING, F. P.—Accelerated Tests for Permanence of Volume of Cement Mortars. *Eng. News, Aug. 24, 1893.*

70. UNWIN, W. C.—On the Rate of Hardening of Cement and Mortar. *Proc. Inst. C. E.*, *Vol. 84, p. 399.*

Vol 27 p 2??

71. WHITTEMORE, D. J.—Tensile Tests of Cement, and an Appliance for More Accurate Determinations. *Trans. Am. Soc. C. E.*, *Vol. 9, p. 329.*
72. WARD, W. E.—Beton Combined with Iron in Buildings. *Trans. Amer. Soc. Mech. Eng.*, *Vol. IV, p. 388.*
73. WEBER, C. O.—The Practical Application of Magnesia Cement. (See paper No. 157.) *Scien. Am. Sup.*, *May 16, 1891.*
74. YARDLEY, E.—Experiments on Cement. *Trans. Am. Soc. C. E.. Vol. 2, p. 153.*
75. GODDARD and EVANS.—Effect of Retempering Cement Mortars. *Eng. News, Jan. 5, 1893.*
76. McCULLOCH, W.—Construction of a Watertight Masonry Dam. *Trans, Am. Soc. C. E., March, 1893.*

VARIOUS NOTES, REVIEWS AND REPORTS.

77. Adulterated Cement Question in Germany. *The Builder, Vol. 42, p. 701.*
78. Anti-freezing Soda Mortar. *Eng. News, Feb. 16, 1893.*
79. Concrete for Harbor Work. *Proc. Inst. C. E., Vol. 87, p. 92.*
80. Concrete in Sea Water. *R. R. Gazette, Vol. 19, p. 570.*
81. Concrete Plant at the Cascades Canal, Oregon. *Eng. News, June 2, 1892.*
82. Concrete in Harbor Work. *Lon. Engineering, Oct. 7, 1892.*
83. Failure of Concrete Piers. *Eng. News, Dec. 11, 1886.*
84. The Hardening of Hydraulic Cement. *Engineer, London, Sept. 21, 1888.*
85. German Specifications for Standard Portland Cement. *Eng. News, Nov. 13, 1886.*
86. Influence of Sea Water on Portland Cement. *Eng. Record, Dec. 26, 1891.*
87. Influence of Sugar upon Cement. *Eng. News, Dec. 24, 1887.*
88. Monier Method of Constructing Arches. *Eng. News, May 23, 1891.*
89. Manufacture of Portland Cement from Slag. *Scientific American Sup., May 31, 1890.*

90. Novel English Portland Cement Plant. *Eng. News, March 21, 1891.*
91. Overburnt Cement. *Lon. Engineer, Dec. 2, 1892.*
92. Portland Cement as a Structural Material. *Engineering Record, Dec. 19, 1891.*
93. Porta Cement Works at Bremen. *Lon. Eng'ng, July 17, 1891.*
94. Report of the Committee on a Uniform System for Tests of Cement. *Trans. Am. Soc. C. E., Vol. 14, p. 475.*
95. Report of Progress of Committee on the Compression of Mortars and Settlement of Masonry. *Trans. Am. Soc. C. E., Vol. 17, p. 213.*
96. Resolutions of the Conferences at Munich and Dresden concerning Uniform Methods of Testing Materials. *Trans. Am. Soc. Mech. Eng., Vol. 11, p. 533.*
97. Tensile Strength of Beton. *Eng. News, May 17, 1890.*
98. Strange Behavior of Cement. *Eng. News, Nov. 26, 1887,* also *Dec. 17, 1887.*

PAPERS IN FRENCH

99. ALEXANDRE, PAUL.—Expériences concernant l'influence du dosage de l'eau sur le résistance des mortiers de ciment. *Annales des Ponts et Chaussées, 1888, Vol. 1, p. 375.*
100. ALEXANDRE, PAUL. —Recherches Expérimentales sur les mortiers hydrauliques. *An. Ponts et Chaus., 1890, Vol. 11, p. 277.*
101. BARREAU.—Les qualités et essais des ciments a prise leute. *An. des Ponts et Chaussées, 1882, Vol. 11, p. 150.*
102. BONNAMI, H.—Étude relative à l'influence de l'alumine sur la résistance des ciments de Portland. *Génie Civil, Vol. 14, p. 180.*
103. BRÜLL, A.—Étude sur les qualitiés du ciment de Portland. *Annales des la construction, 1881, col 150.*
104. CANDLOT, E.—Note contenant les résultats d'expériences faites sur le ciment de Portland gâché au chlorure de calcium. *Annales de la construction, 1886, col 171.*

105. CANDLOT, E.—Note sur l'emploi des materiaux hydrauliques. *Annales de la Construction, 1889.*

106. CANDLOT, E.—Note sur la prise et le durcissement des mortiers de ciment de Portland. *An. de la Con.. 1888.*

107. DEVAL.—Essais a l'eau chaude des ciments et chaux hydrauliques. *Annales Industrielles, 1890, Vol. 2, p. 408.* (See also paper No. 137.)

108. DOLOT.—Note sur l'action du gypse sur les mortiers. *An. de la Construction, 1888, col. 11.*

109. DURAND-CLAYE AND DEBRAY.—Étude sur les ciments Magnesiens. *An. des Ponts et Chaussées, 1886, Vol. 1, p. 845.*

110. DURAND-CLAYE AND DEBRAY.—La dilatation des pâtes de ciment de Portland. *An. des Ponts et Chaussées, 1888, Vol. 1, p. 810.*

111. DURAND-CLAYE AND DEBRAY.— Perméabilité des mortiers de ciments Portland. *An. des Ponts et Chaus., 1888, Vol. 1, p. 816.* (See paper No. 19.)

112. FERET, R.— Diverses Expériences concernant les ciments. *An. des Ponts et Chaussées, 1890, Vol. 1, p. 313.*

113. FERET, R.—Sur la compacité des mortiers hydrauliques. *An. des Ponts et Chaussées, 1892, Vol. 2, p. 5.*

114. FOY, J.—Étude sur les ciments de Laitier. *Annales Industrielles, 1887, Vol. 2, p. 724.*

115. FOY, J.—Étude sur les ciments siliceux. *Annales Industrielles, 1888, Vol. 2, p. 814.*

116. GROSCLAUDE, J.—Étude sur la fabrication et les propriétés du ciment de laitier. *Annales Industrielles, 1889, Vol. 2, p. 89.*

117. GOBIN, A.— Fabrication des chaux hydrauliques. *An. des Ponts et Chaussées, 1887, Vol. 2, p. 464.*

118. GOBIN, A —Étude sur les ciments de l'Isére. *An. des Ponts et Chaussées, 1889, Vol. 1, p. 755.*

119. LECHARTIER.—Influence de la magnésie dans les ciments dits de Portland. *An. de la Construction, 1886.*

120. LECHATELIER, H.— Recherches expérimentelles sur la constitution des Ciments. *Annales des Ponts et Chaussées, 1882, Vol. 1, p. 482.*

121. LeChatelier, H. — Recherches experimentelles sur la constitution des Mortiers hydrauliques. *Annales des Mines, 1887, Vol. I, p. 345.* (See paper No. 37.)

122. Perrodil. — Sur la marche du durcissement des Mortiers. *An. des Ponts et Chausées, 1884, Vol. 1, p. 592.*

123. Prost, M. A. — La fabrication et les propriétés des ciments de laitier. *Annales des Mines, 1889, Vol. 2, p. 158.*

124. Vicat. — Étude sur la pouzzolane. *An. des Ponts et Chaussées, 1836, Vol. 2, p. 96.*

125. Vicat. — Ponzzolanes artificielles. *An. des Ponts et Chaus., 1842, Part 2, p. 135.*

126. Vicat. — Influence de l'eau de mer sur les Mortiers de pouzzolane artificielle. *An. des Ponts et Chaus., 1843, p. 232.*

127. Vicat. — Mortiers à la mer. *An. des Ponts et Chaus., 1854, Vol. 2, p. 8.*

PAPERS IN GERMAN.

128. Bauschinger, J. — Verhandlungen der Münchener conferenz und von ihr Gewahlten Ständigen Commission zur Vereinbarung einheitlicher Prüfungsmethoden fur Bau- und Constructions-Materielen. *Mittheilingen aus dem Mechanisch-Technischen Laboratorium, Munich, No. 16.*

129. Bohm. — Ueber das System Monier. *Civil ingenieur, 1891, p. 474.*
    Bohme. — *Mittheilungen aus dem K. technischen Versuchsaustalten, Berlin.*

130. *1885, p. 78.* — Ueber den Einfluss der Zusätz von verschiedenen pulverformigen Substanzen auf Portland-Cemente.

131. *1885, p. 93.* — Untersuchung der cemente auf Volumbeständigkeit nach verschiedenen Methoden.

132. *1886, p. 50.* — Einfluss des Frostes bei mit Schlackenzusatz versehenen Portland-Cementen.

133. *1887, p. 108.* Ueber die abnutzbarkeit der Cemente und verschiedener Mörtel Ausdenselben.

134. *1889, p. 43.* — Ueber den Einfluss des Frostes auf die Festigkeit der Cement.

135. BUSCH, A.—Mittheilungen aus der Cement-Technik. *Dinglers Polytechnisches Journnl, Vol. 282, p. 116.*

136. DELBRUCK-STETTIN.—Methoden der Untersuchung des Cements. *Z. des Vereins Deutschen Ing., 1885, p. 712.*

137. DEVAL. — Heifswasser Prüfungen für Cemente. *Thonindustrie Zeitung, Vol. 15, p. 384.* (See paper 107.)

138. DYCKERHOFF, R.—Wirkung der Magnesia in gebrannten Cement. *Thon. Zeit., Vol. 14, p. 452.*

139. DYCKERHOFF, R.—Ueber die Verfälschung von Cement. *Ding. Poly. Jour., Vol. 248, p. 245.*

140. ERDMENGER. — Kochen von Cementproben mit Hochdruckdampf. *Thonindustrie Zeit., Vol. 15, p. 65.*

141. ELBERS. — Verwertung von Hochofenschlacken. *Zeitschrift des Vereins D. Ing., 1885, p. 1022.*

142. FRESENIUS.—Portland-Cement und Nachweis fremder Zusätze zu demselben. *Thon. Zeit., Vol. 9, p. 71.*

143. FRESENIUS.—Untersuchung über den Nachweis von Verfalschungen im Portland-Cement. *Thon. Zeit., Vol. 8, p. 231.*

144. GARY, M.—Abnutzbarkeit von Cement und Cementmörtelu. *Thonindustrie Zeitung, Vol. 15, p. 233.*

145. GRAUER.—Wirkung der Magnesia in Portland-Cement. *Thou. Zeit., Vol. 15, p. 659.* Abstract in *Dinglers, Vol. 282, p. 120.*

146. KOSMAN.—Ueber die Binding der Kalkerde in Hochofenschlacken und Portlandcement. *Dinglers Polytechnisches Jour., Vol. 271, p. 138.*

147. KNAPP. —Hochofenschlacke und Portlandcement. *Dingler's Poly. Jour., Vol. 265, p. 184.*

148. MANSKE.—Cement und dessen Verfälschung. *Z. des Vereins D. Ing., 1885, p. 921.*

149. PHILLIPP AND BELELUBSKY.—Technische Bedmgungen aus die annahme von Portland zementen bei Arbeiten in Ressort des russischen Ministeriums der Wegekommunikalionen. *Civilingenieur, 1892, p. 569.*

150. PINKENBURG. —Schlackencemeut. *Thon. Zeit., Vol. 14, p. 768.*

151. SCHULATSCHENKO. — Nomenclatur der Luft und Wasser-Mortel. *Civilingenieur, 1886, p. 561.*

152. TAKAYAMA, J. Ueber den Gebrauch des zersetzen Granitsandes als natüralichen Mörtel in Japan. *Dinglers Poly. Jour., Vol. 278, p. 275.*

153. TETMAJOR.—Lufttreibende Portland-Cement und die Darrprobe. *Pamphlet, Zurich.*

154. TETMAJOR.—Schlackencement. *Thon. Zeit., Vol. 10, p. 177.*

155. TETMAJOR.— Ueber die Volumenbeständigkeit hydraulischer Bindemittel. *Thon. Zeit., Vol. 11, p. 443.*

156. TETMAJOR.—Bericht der Subcommission No. 12 der zweiten Standigen Commission zur Vereinbarung einheitlicher Prüfungsmethoden fur Bau und Constructions-Materialen. *Pamphlet, Zurich, 1889.*

157. WEBER, C. O.— Praktische Verwendung von Magnesia-Cement. (See paper No. 73.) *Thon. Zeit., Vol. 15, p. 341.*

158. ZSIGMONDY.—Ueber die Untersuchung und das Verhalten von Cement. *Dinglers Jour., Vol. 273, p. 551.*

159. ZSIGMONDY.—Ueber Hochofenschlacken und deren Verwerthung. *Dinglers Poly. Jour., Vol. 284, p. 233.*

160. ZSIGMONDY.— Ueber den Werth von Heisswasserproben bei der Prüfung von Cement und hydraulischen Kalk. *Dinglers Poly. Jour., Vol. 280, p 182.*

161. ZSIGMONDY.—Ueber die Untersuchung und das Verhalten von Cement. *Dinglers Journal, Vol. 281, p. 114.*

VARIOUS NOTES, REPORTS AND REVIEWS.

162. Bestimmung des Oesterreichischen Ingenieur- und Architekten-Vereins, die einheitliche Prüfung und Lieferung von Portland-Zement betreffend. *Civilingenieur, Vol. 36, p. 135.* Abstract *Dinglers, Vol. 281, p. 90.*

163. Ueber die Herstellung und Untersuchung von Cement. *Dinglers Poly. Jour., Vol. 261, p. 344 and p. 529.*

164. Zur Kentuiss des Cements. *Dinglers Poly. Jour., Vol. 233, p. 222, and p. 387.*

VERHANDLUNGEN DES VEREINS DEUTSCHEN
ZEMENTFABRIKANTEN.

165. *Zeit. des Vereins D. Ing.*, *1886, p. 832 and p. 854.*
166.   "   "   "   *1887, p. 738.*
167.   "   "   "   *1888, p. 710.*
168.   "   "   "   *1890, p. 1353 and p. 1383.*
169.   "   "   "   *1891, p. 374.*
170.   "   "   "   *1892, p. 1054.*

ART. 32. TOPICAL REFERENCES TO PAPERS.

In the list of literature in Art. 31, only the titles of the papers are given. As nearly all the papers mentioned are of value in a general study of the subject of cements, and the list is not large, it is thought unnecessary to add any explanation or comment.

In order, however, to aid in classifying the references, a topical index is here appended, indicating, for each of a few prominent headings, the papers in which the subject mentioned is most fully discussed.

The papers in Art. 31 are numbered consecutively, and are here referred to by number:

TOPICAL INDEX.

Manufacture of Portland Cement. Papers, 4, 12, 20, 24, 48, 58, 59, 65, 90, 91, 93, 101, 112, 151, 163.
Manufacture of Natural Cement. Papers, 11, 20, 27, 50, 55, 58, 118, 151.
Chemical Theory. Composition. Papers 5, 11, 12, 16, 17, 18, 37, 38, 42, 43, 49, 65, 67, 73, 79, 91, 100, 101, 102, 104, 108, 109, 110, 112, 114, 115, 119, 120, 122, 123, 130, 135, 137, 138, 141, 143, 145, 146, 147, 151, 161, 164.

Adulteration of Cement. Papers 77, 112, 130. 132, 139, 142, 143, 146, 147, 148, 151, 161.

Manufacture of Slag Cement. Papers 20, 28, 60, 89, 114, 116, 117, 123, 141, 146, 147, 151, 154, 159, 163.

Properties of Portland Cement. Papers 16, 31, 35, 38, 43, 44, 49, 79, 84, 91, 101, 102, 103, 104, 105, 109, 112, 115, 119, 122, 128, 137, 143, 145, 146, 147, 156, 163, 164.

Properties of Natural Cement. Papers 11, 33, 35, 38, 43, 50, 55, 73, 79, 84, 105, 109, 115, 118, 137, 156, 164.

Properties of Slag Cement. Papers 28, 38, 43, 60, 79, 84, 114, 116, 123, 132, 135, 146, 147, 154, 163.

Soundness. Permanence of Volume. Papers 17, 21, 23, 24, 29, 38, 43, 49, 67, 69, 73, 79, 80, 85, 86, 94, 96, 98, 100, 102, 104, 106, 107, 108, 109, 110, 112, 113, 116, 119, 131, 135, 136, 137, 140, 143, 145, 153, 155, 156, 160, 161, 167, 168.

Methods of Testing. Papers, 8, 14, 15, 17, 18, 21, 23, 24, 29, 31, 38, 39, 42, 43, 45, 54, 61, 62, 63, 68, 69, 71, 85, 94, 96, 100, 101, 104, 107, 112, 119, 121, 131, 128, 136, 143, 148, 149, 153, 156, 161, 162, 163, 164, 165.

Microscopic Examination. Papers, 8, 37, 112, 120.

Heat Tests. Papers, 17, 23, 24, 29, 38, 43, 69, 85, 107, 110, 131, 137, 140, 153, 156, 160, 161.

Use in Mortar and Concrete. Papers. 2, 3, 6, 7, 9, 13, 14, 25, 32, 33, 34, 35, 36, 40, 41, 42, 46, 47, 49, 51, 52, 53, 61, 64, 66, 72, 76, 79, 80, 82, 83, 88, 97, 99, 100, 105, 106, 108, 113, 129, 135, 158, 164, 169.

Effect of Sea Water. Papers, 1, 14, 25, 29, 38, 47, 49, 67, 79, 80, 82, 86, 100, 102, 105, 106, 109, 110, 113, 115, 119, 131, 135, 138.

Permeability of Mortar. Papers, 1, 19, 26, 33, 49, 76, 79, 100, 111, 113, 161, 168.

Effect of Freezing.—Use of Salt. Papers, 9, 10, 42, 53a, 57, 76, 78, 132, 134, 158, 163, 167.

Retempering Mortar. Papers, 14, 32, 75, 100.